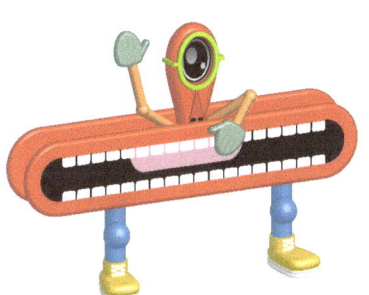

For the possible,
not the probable.

All the characters and concepts in this book are registered and protected on WGAW Registry #2169418.

All rights reserved. No part of this book may be reproduced by any mechanical, photographic or electronic process, or in the form of a phonographic recording; nor may it be stored in a retrieval system, transmitted or otherwise be copied for public or private use other than for fair use as brief quotations embodied in articles and reviews, without prior written permission of the publisher.

Characters with character
By Markus Baker

Published by R-and-Q.com
Copyright © 2021
Mark Markus Baker

ISBN: 978-1-9163571-7-4

CHARACTERS WITH

CHARACTER

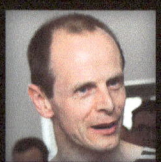

INTRODUCTION

How this book and the characters in it appeared in our lives.

Having sold everything I owned, the car, the house and all my belongings. I decided to quit my job and travel the world.

With a degree in visual communication and having designed for the film industry and then a tech startup, I was ready to design and create for a different reason. As I circumnavigated the globe I wanted to design for myself with no consideration of clients, money or conformity. The plan was to develop ideas that sparked my creativity and made my heart sing.

So, this is what I did as I travelled through Russia, Mongolia, China, Vietnam, South Korea, Japan, The Philippines, Canada, India, UAE, USA, Israel, Palestine and Jordan.

The creative outcomes of these experiences, which include staying in a Buddhist temple and with a Taoist master in the hills of South Korea, are the characters you are about to meet in this book. Most of whom were found hiding as everyday objects in one of the countries I visited.

If any of these characters inspire you and you wish to discuss them further, please do get in touch.

Best wishes

Markus

www.R-and-Q.com

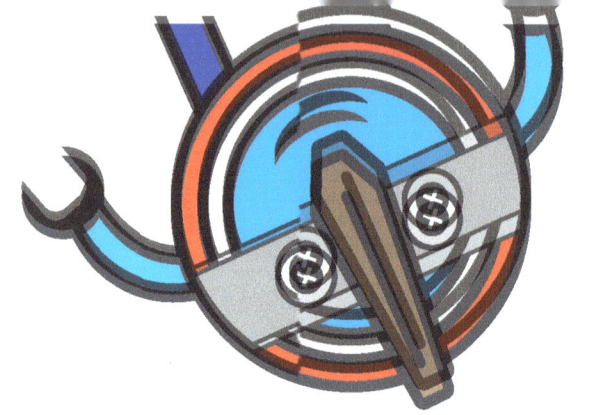
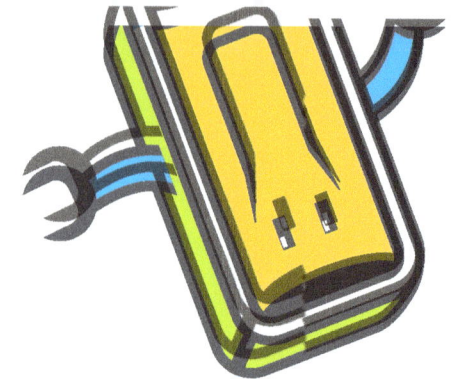
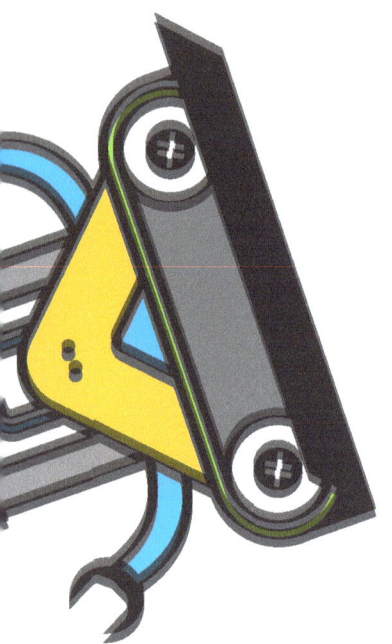
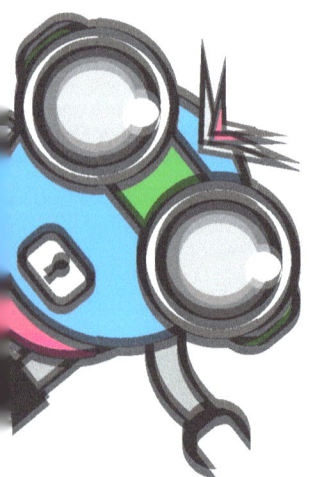
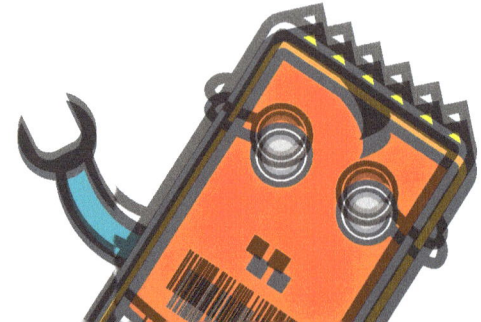
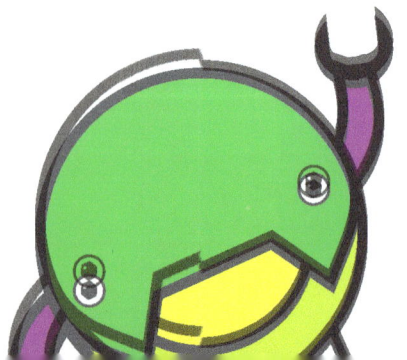

On Calma, an island far away, but nearer than you think, live the Mettas.

The Mettas are a set of characters created from faces in everyday objects.

Each Metta has a unique kind, caring & gentle superpower.

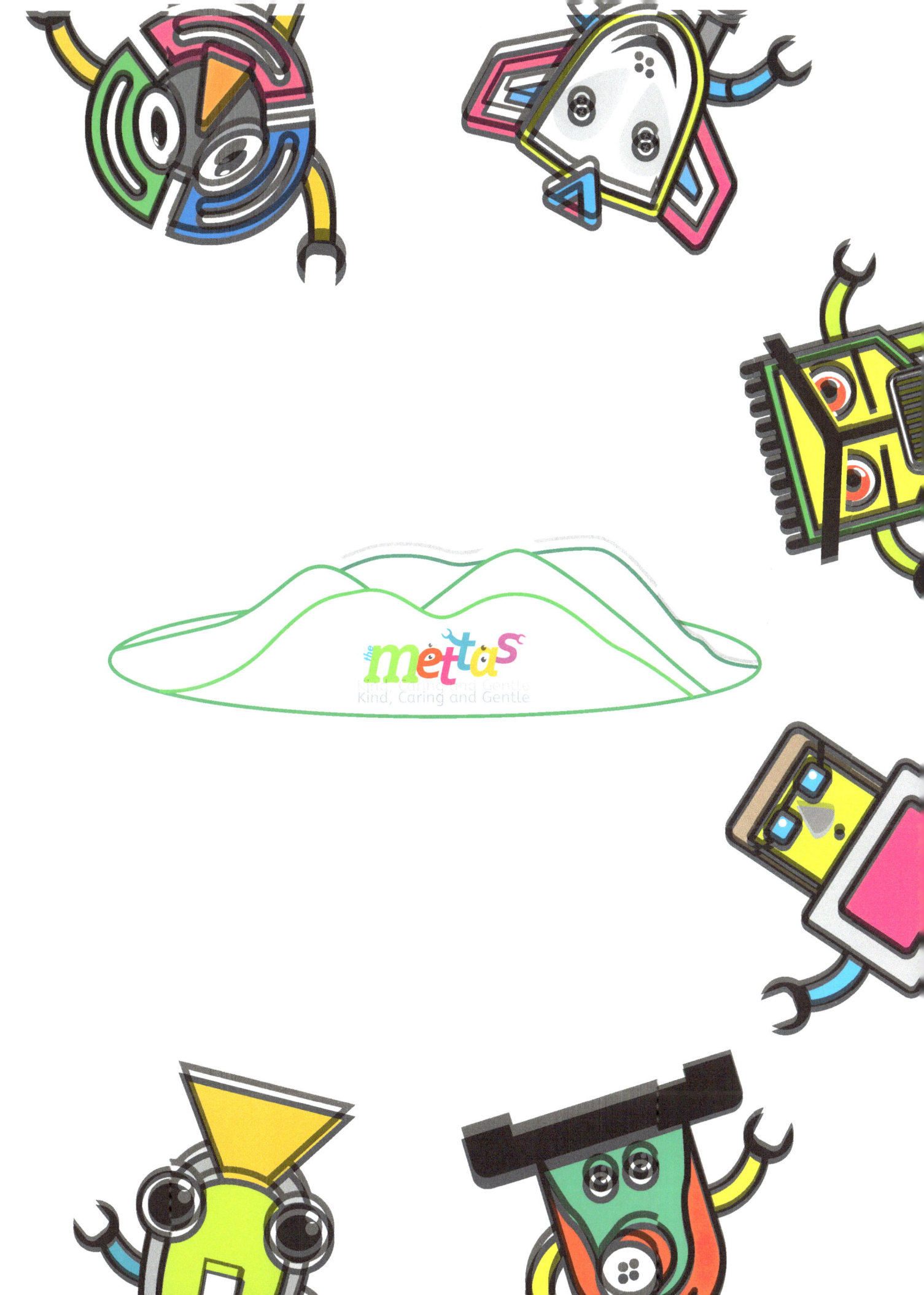

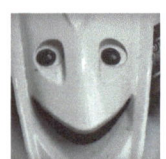# SCOOT...
...was discovered on the front of a moped in Vietnam.

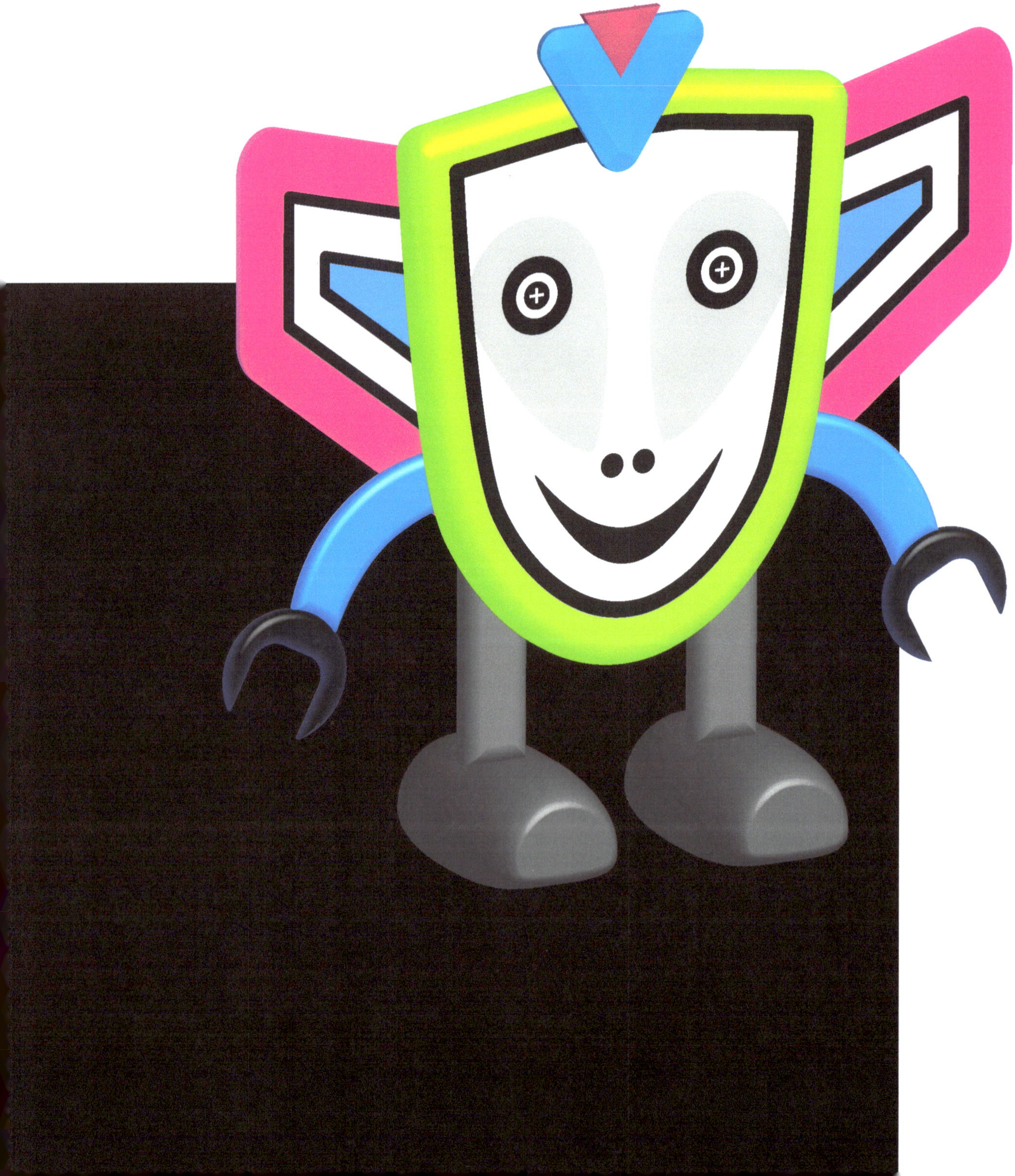

Reason for name:
Mopeds are sometimes known as Scooters, so Scoot became this happy characters name.

Scoot's Character:
With one mouth and two ears, Scoot believes that we learn more by listening than we do by talking.

Scoot's Superpower:
Teaching us the power of listening and not judging others, Scoot realises we are all trying to do the best we can in this life.

MOPPY...

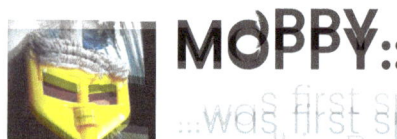

...was first spotted leaning against a wall in Boracay, Philippines.

Reason for name:
Moppy's name is because this character is based on a floor cleaning mop.

Moppy's Character:
When trying to make others sad, Moppy learns a lesson about kindness from one of the other Mettas, leading us to see the kinder, happier and gentler side of Moppy.

Moppy's Superpower:
Moppy shows us that kindness always wins, sharing that although we may sometimes do bad things, it does not make us a bad person because in a similar situation in the future we can always choose to behave in a kinder way.

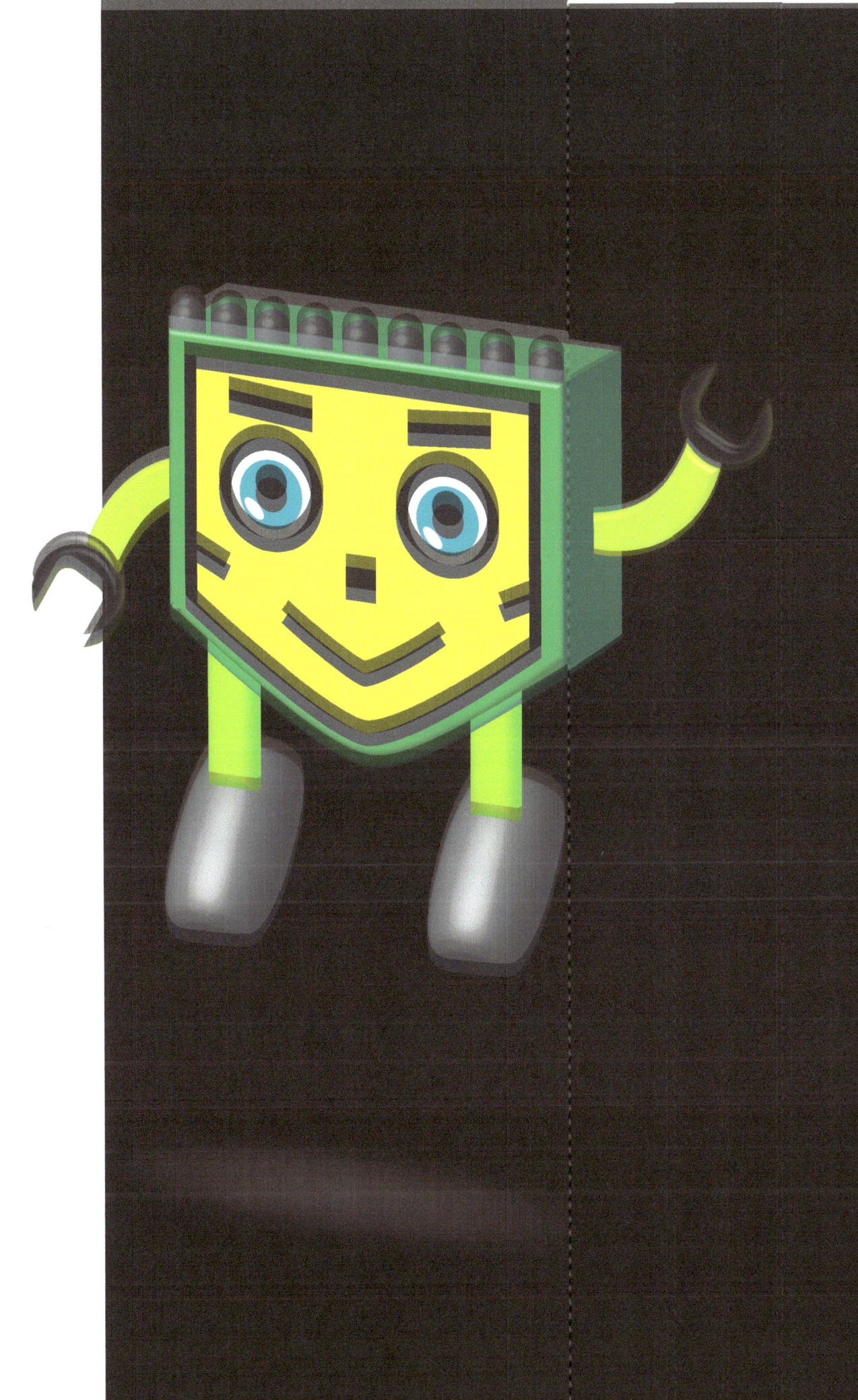

SHIFT...

...was discovered whilst locking a door in Vancouver, Canada.

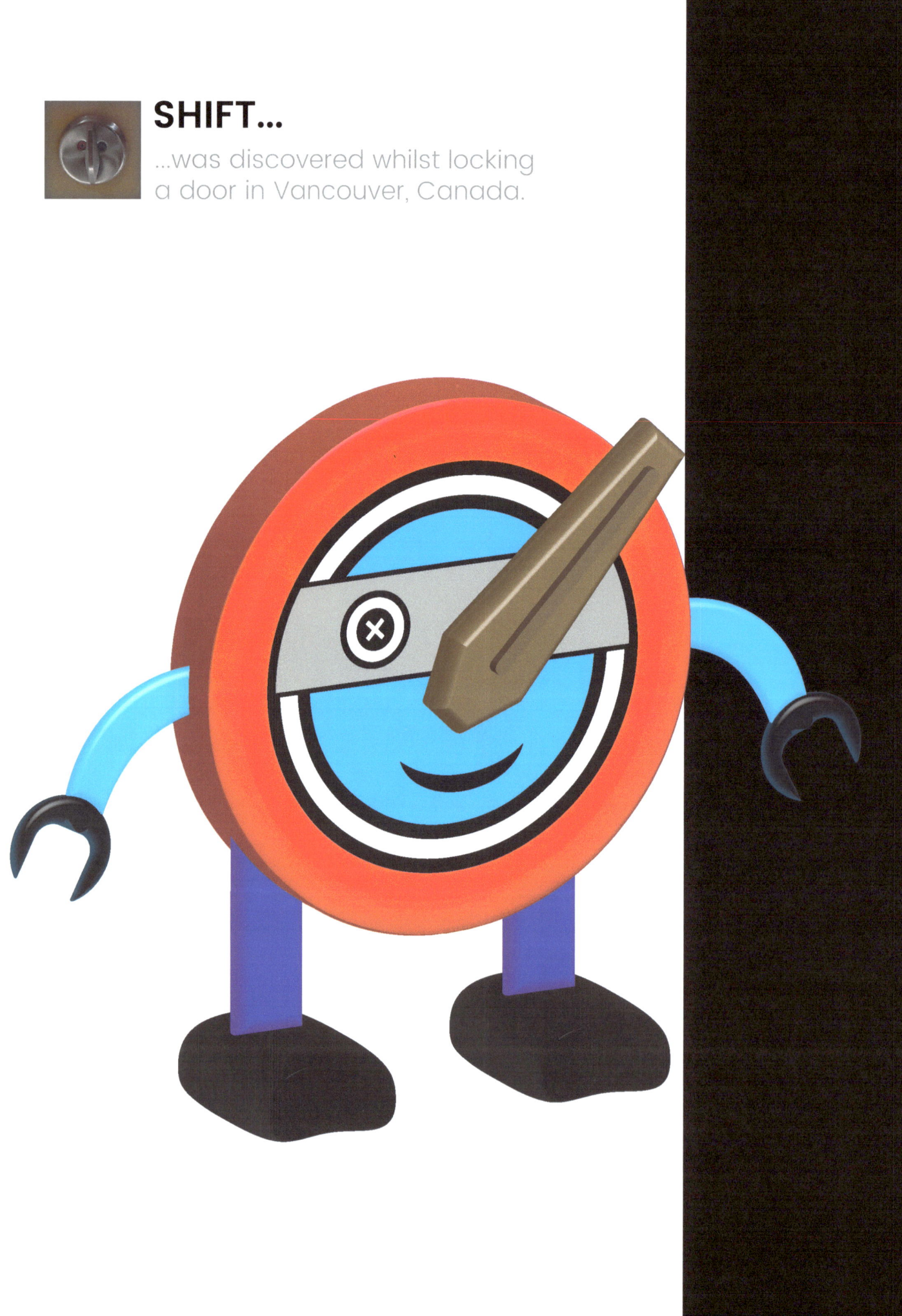

Reason for name:
We can 'Shift' a lock from locked to unlocked.

Shift's Character:
Shift is great at looking at every situation from different perspectives by moving the nose to cover each eye to check everyone is treated fairly.

Shift's Superpower:
Making sure everything is as fair and just as possible.

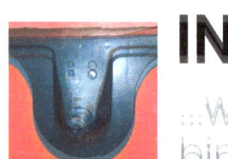

INA:::
...was discovered on the side of a wheelie bin in Boston, Lincolnshire in the UK.

Reason for name:
Ina looks like a Bull, which links to the saying a Bull 'in a' china shop.

Ina's Character:
Either manically rushing around or chilled, calm and in the moment, there is no middle ground with Ina.

Ina's Superpower:
Using breathing exercises and techniques to slow down and improve both performance and relaxation.

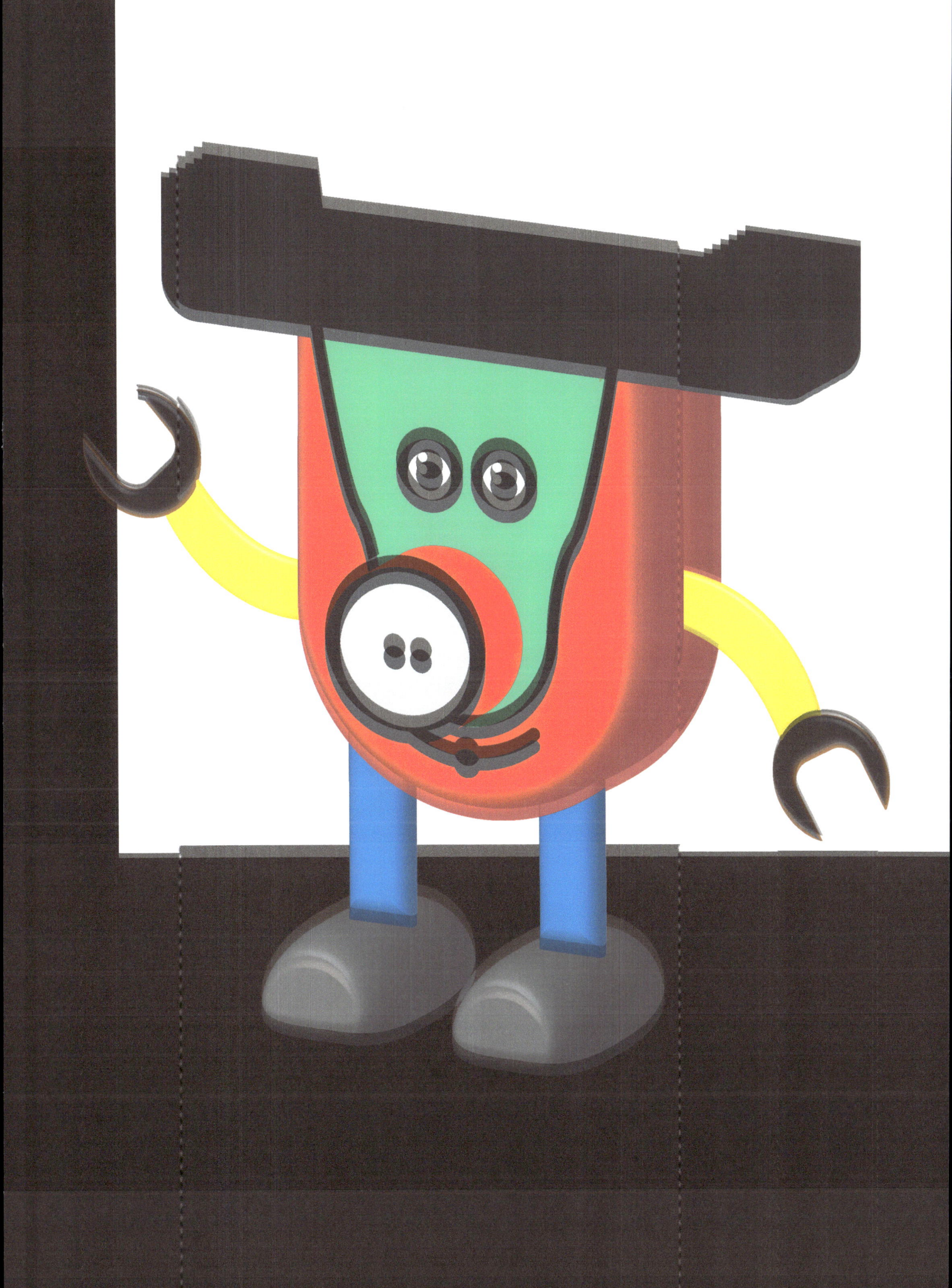

BEAM...

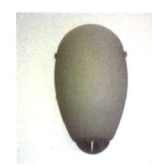

...was discovered as a wall light in a hostel in Vancouver, Canada.

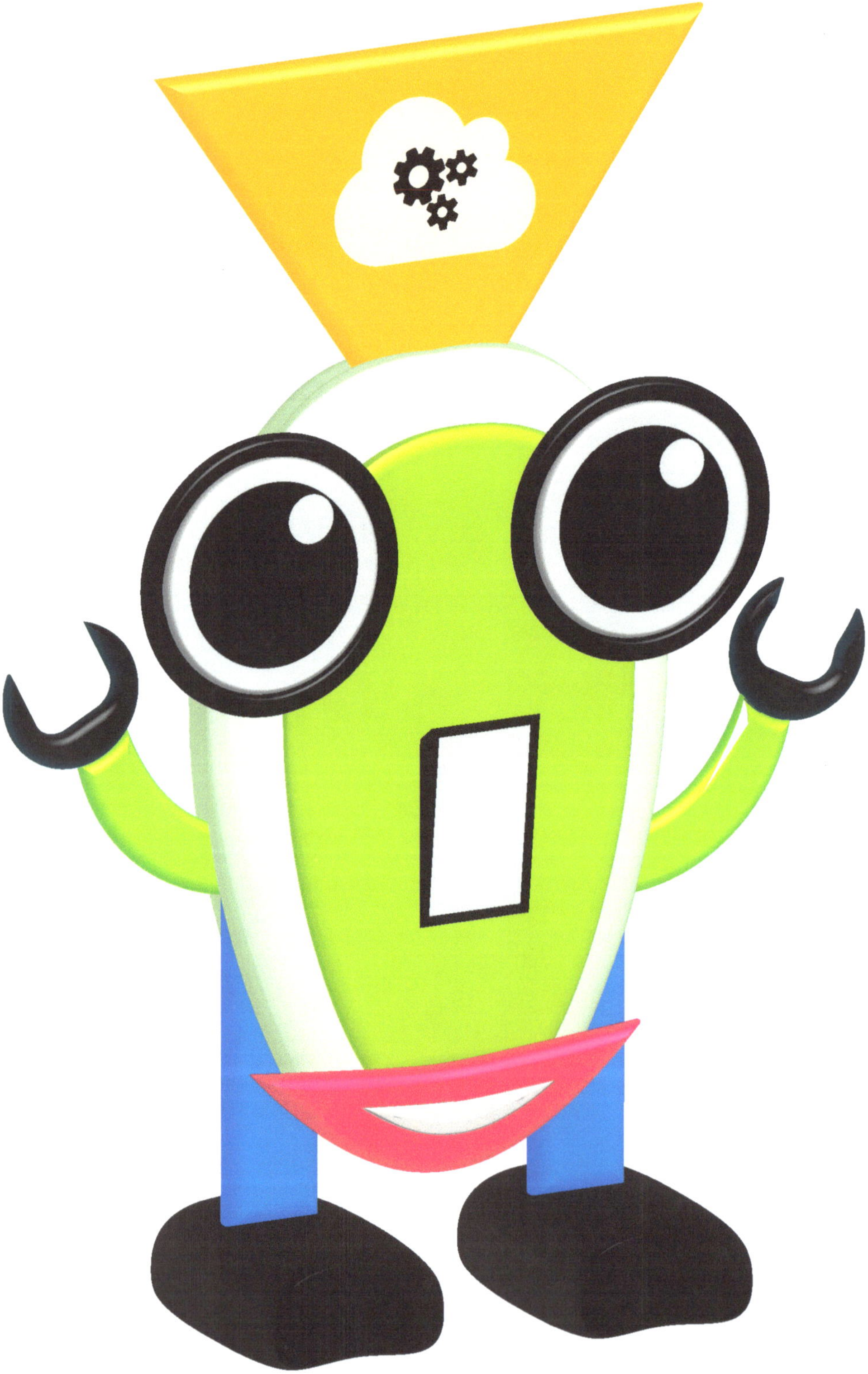

Reason for name:
Beam's name links both to light and the emotion of happiness, like a beaming smile.

Beam's Character:
When Beam's light switch nose is activated, a big yellow beam of light comes from the top of the head, showing all the thoughts Beam is having.

Beam's Superpower:
By being mindful by watching thoughts without getting too involved with them, Beam is great at teaching meditation.

LENS...

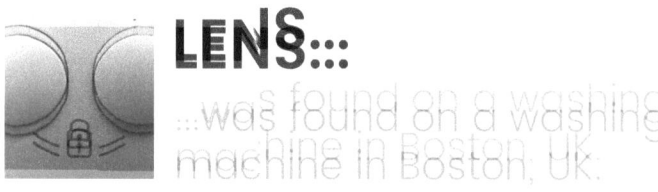

...was found on a washing machine in Boston, UK.

Reason for name:
The buttons on the washing machine are like lenses in a pair of glasses.

Lens' Character:
Always seeing the bright side of life regardless of how bad it gets, Lens can find the positive in any situation.

Lens' Superpower:
Finding the good in everyone and everything, Lens helps the other Mettas to be happy & free from suffering.

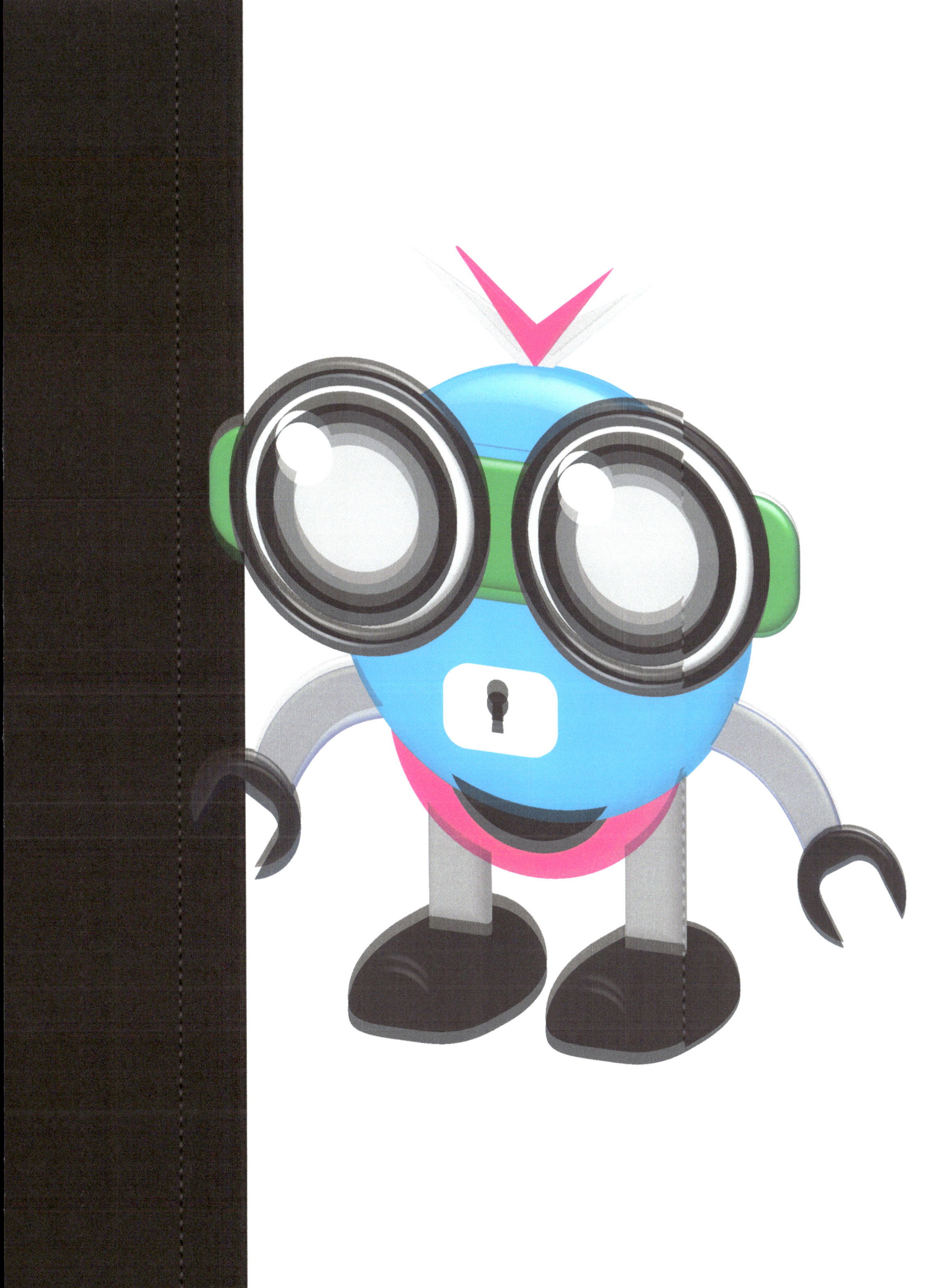

GLOW...

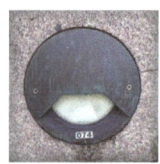

...was found as a light along the Cheong-gye-cheon stream in Seoul, South Korea.

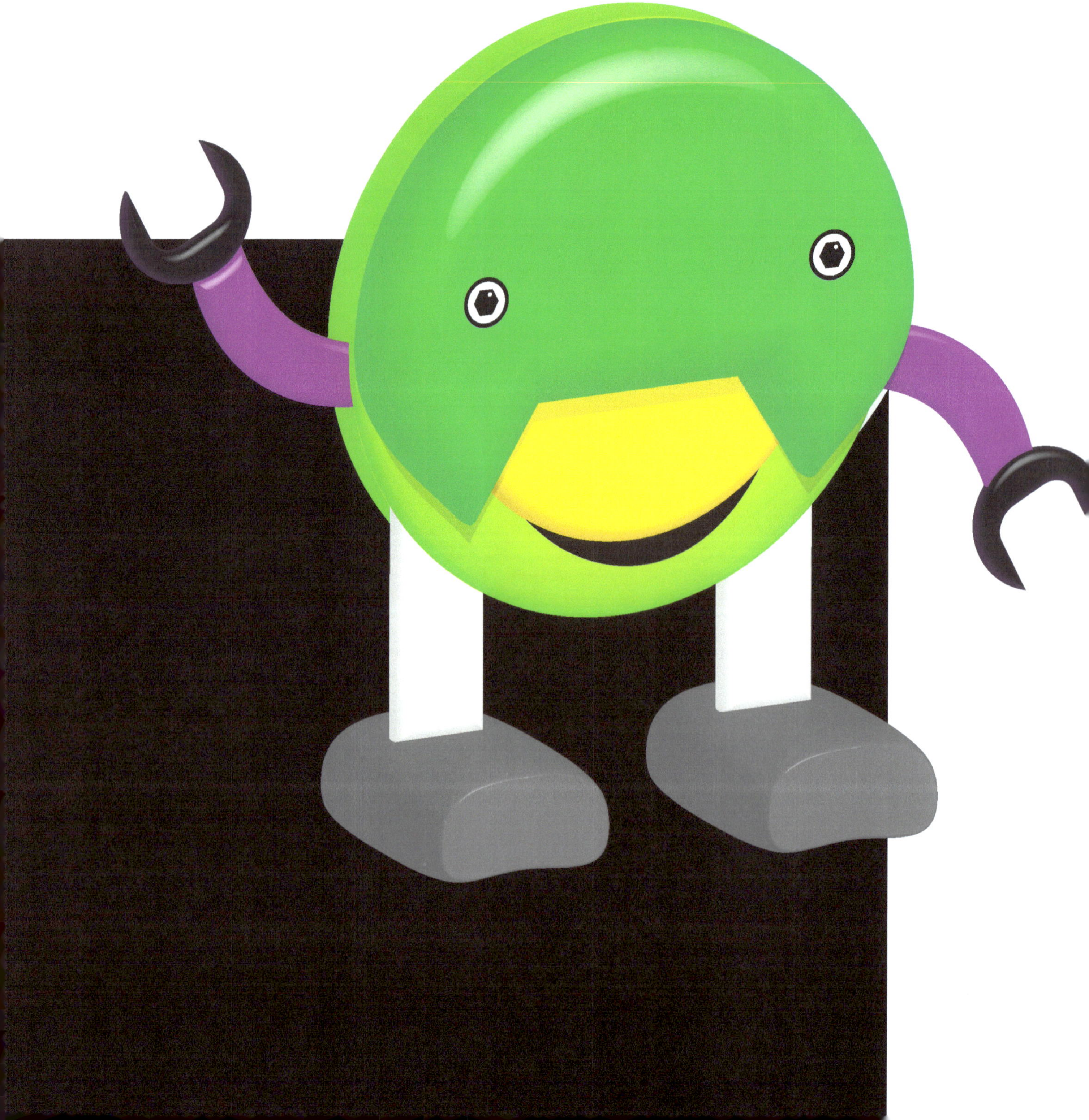

Reason for name:
A light can guide us with its 'Glow'. We may also be glowing after helping others.

Glow's Character:
Most of the time Glow is chilled and emotionally honest. However, like a duck, looking calm on the surface with the legs kicking wildly underneath, Glow can try and hide feelings and emotions.

Glow's Superpower:
Guiding others to get the help they need.

CHIP...

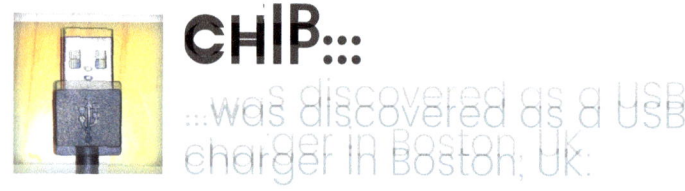

...was discovered as a USB charger in Boston, UK.

Reason for name:
Named after the Microchips that are used in most of our technology.

Chip's Character:
Embraces all the new tech that helps us improve our emotional well-being.

Chip's Superpower:
Sharing how technology can help us become more mindful. Technology like virtual reality, biofeedback, online videos, audio and apps.

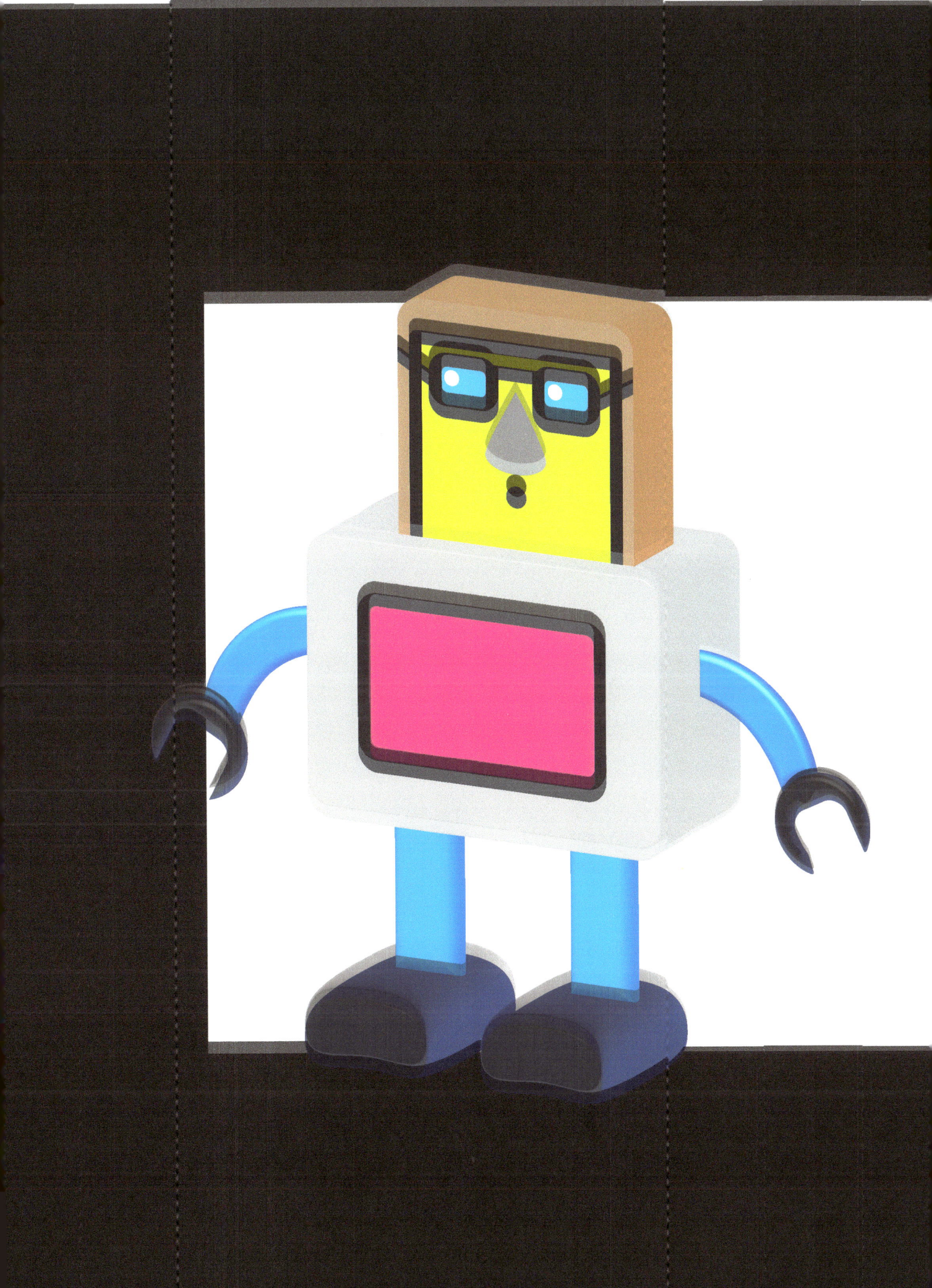

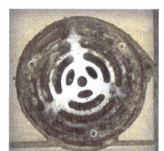

SPIN...

...was found as a drain in a shower in Toronto, Canada.

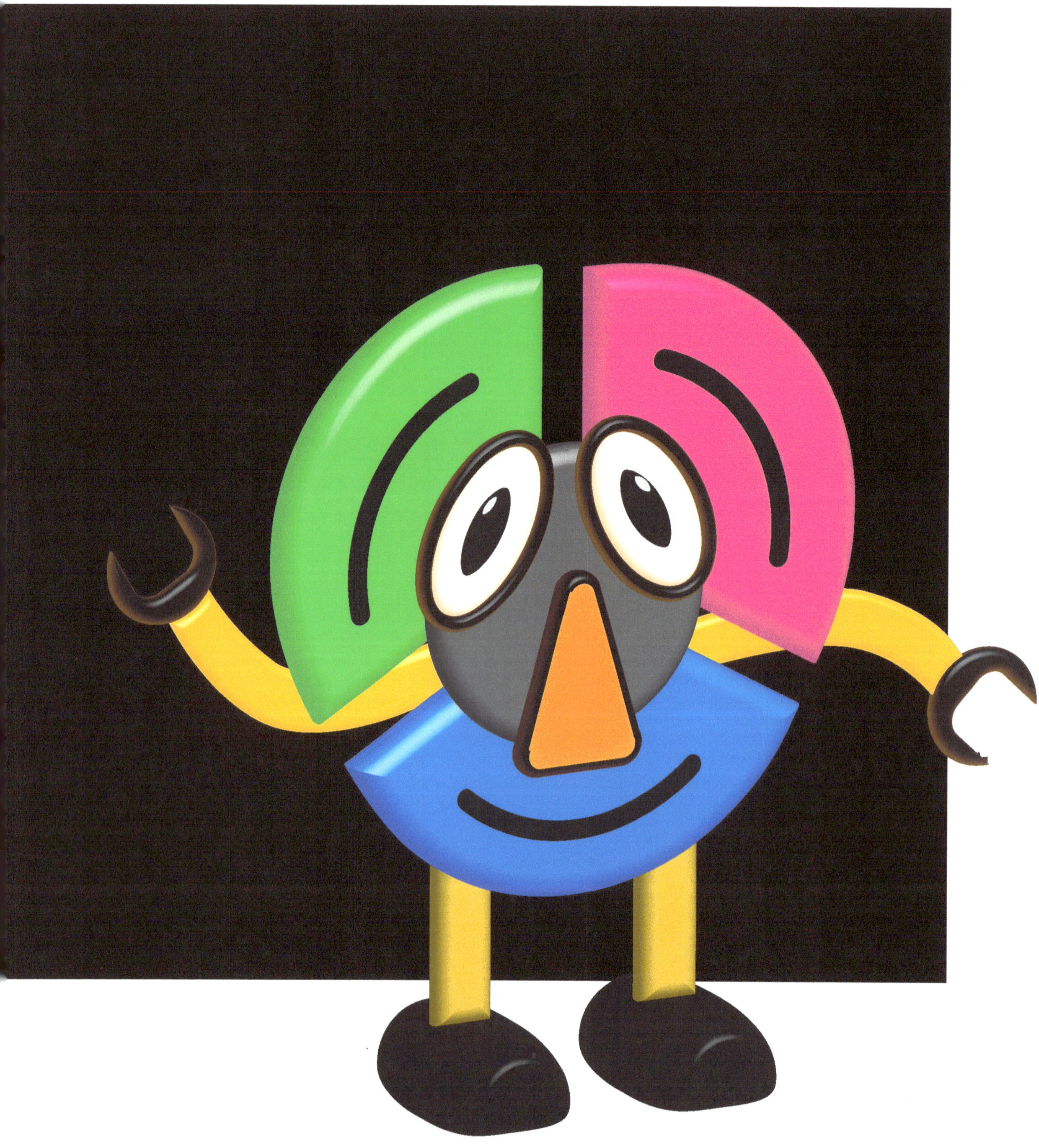

Reason for name:
Emotionally, like water going down a drain, we can feel in a 'Spin'.

Spin's Character:
Being very considerate and empathetic, Spin always thinks before speaking by asking the following three questions: Are the words true, necessary and kind? Spin speaks the truth with the green mouth, the necessary with the blue mouth and kindness with the pink mouth.

Spin's Superpower:
Along with how to be kind, Spin encourages us to ask the three questions before we speak, thus sharing the power and effect our words can have on others.

TIG...

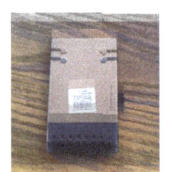

...was discovered hiding as a notebook in Peterborough, UK.

Reason for name:
This notebook was purchased from a shop called Tiger, so Tig felt like the right name for this character.

Tig's Character:
Due to the habit of always noting everything down, Tig has a fantastic memory. Tig loves listing things; things to do, top 10 favourite things and things not to forget.

Tig's Superpower:
How to improve our memory with helpful techniques and stories.

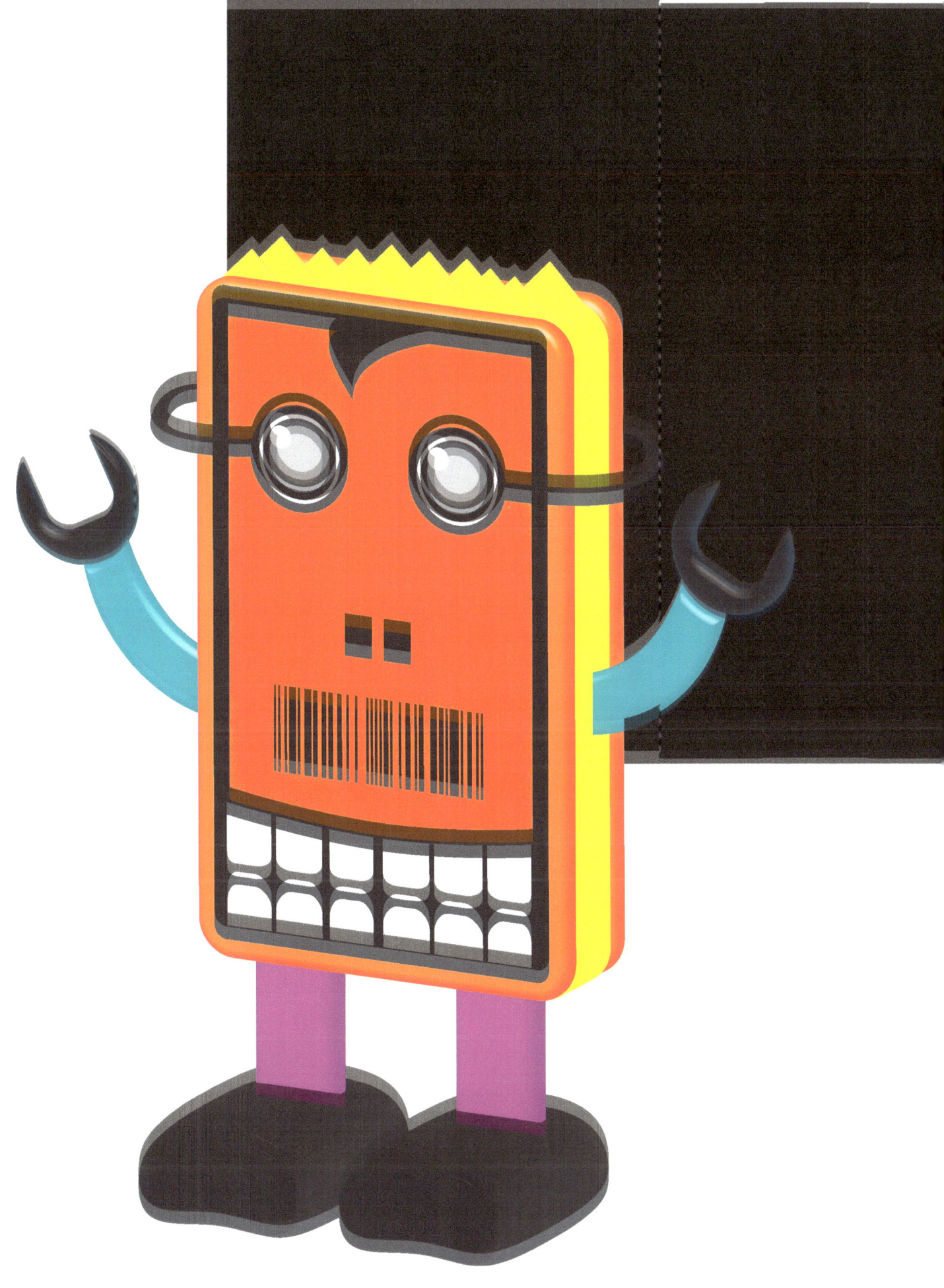

GEE...

...was discovered as a squeegee in a bathroom in Boston, UK.

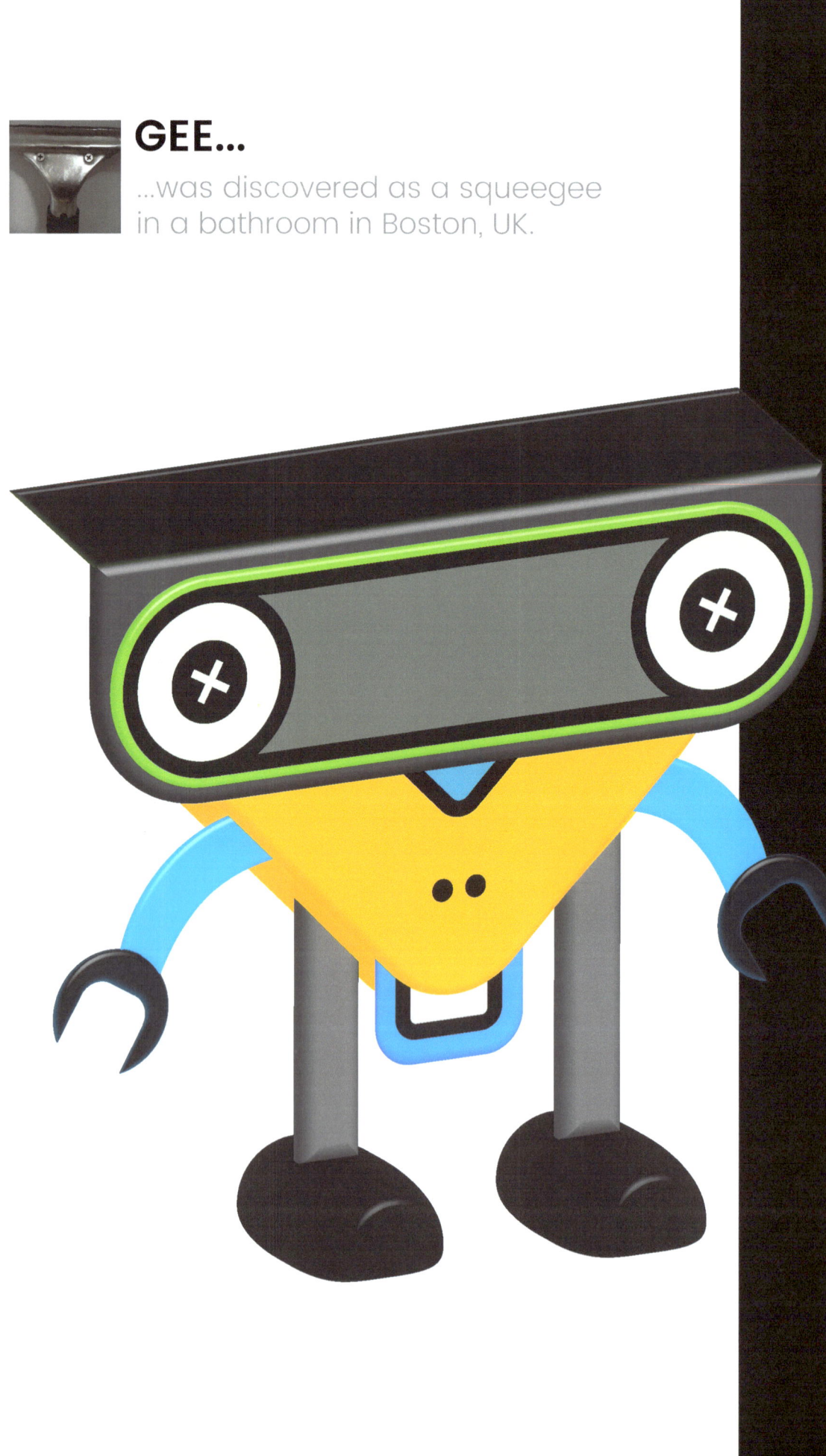

Reason for name:
Taking the 'Gee' from the word squeegee, this character's name also has a positive feeling as in 'Gee, I am happy!'

Gee's Character:
Doing everything with complete focus and concentration, Gee loves to be fully mindful in every moment.

Gee's Superpower:
Sharing how we can develop mindfulness, patience and awareness with focus and concentrate.

SERVI:::

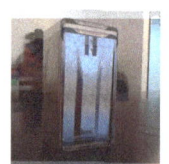

...was found as a napkin dispenser in a hostel in Vancouver, Canada.

Reason for name:
Napkins are sometimes called serviettes in the UK and servi is always of service to others.

Servi's Character:
Loving to help others, servi has to be careful not to become drained and emotionally empty.

Servi's Superpower:
Teaching that it is ok to speak about feelings, thoughts and emotions.

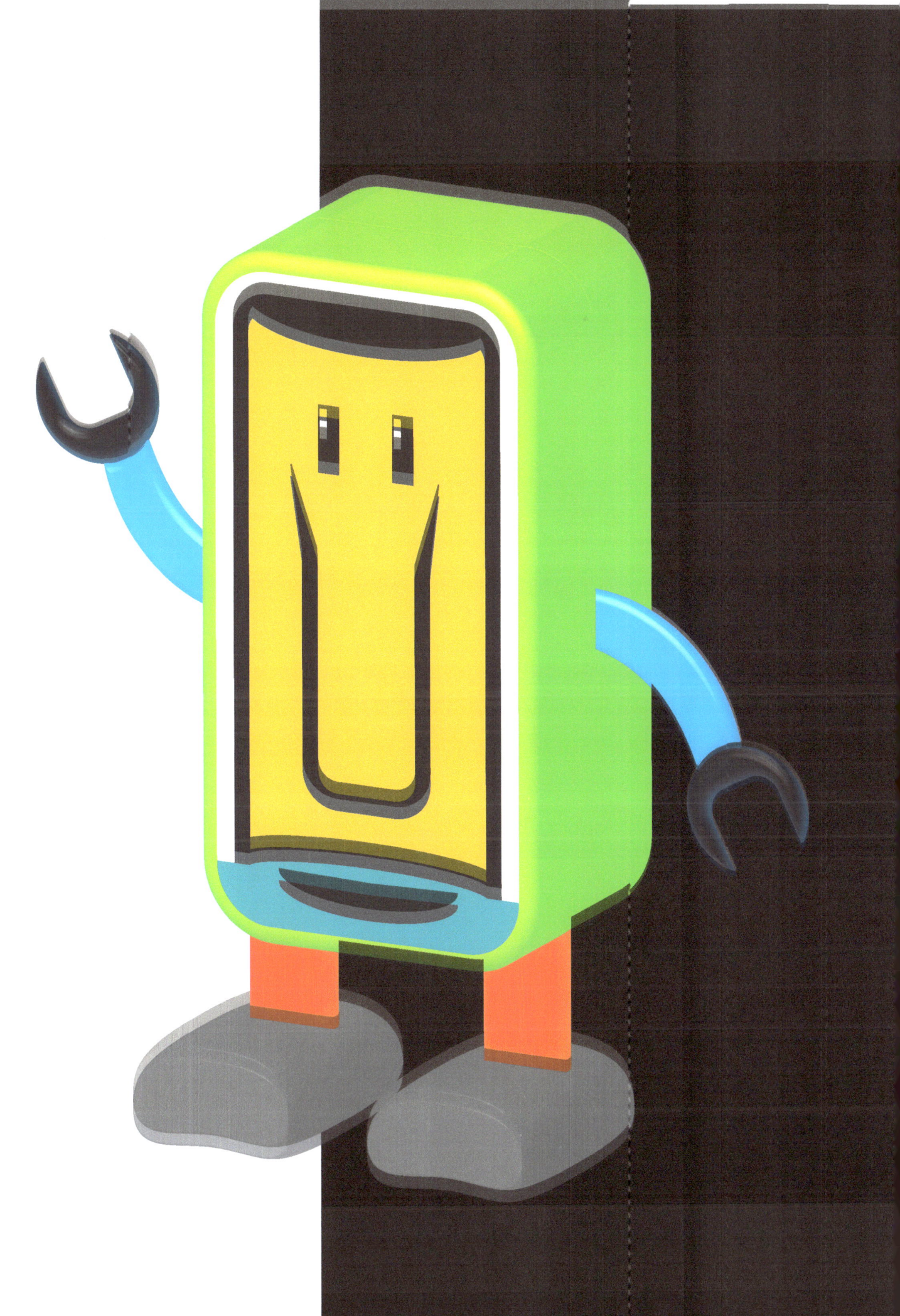

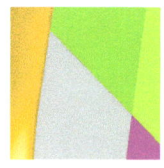# THE WAG BOARD

The Mettas use this multifunctional board to travel on water, in the air and on the ground.

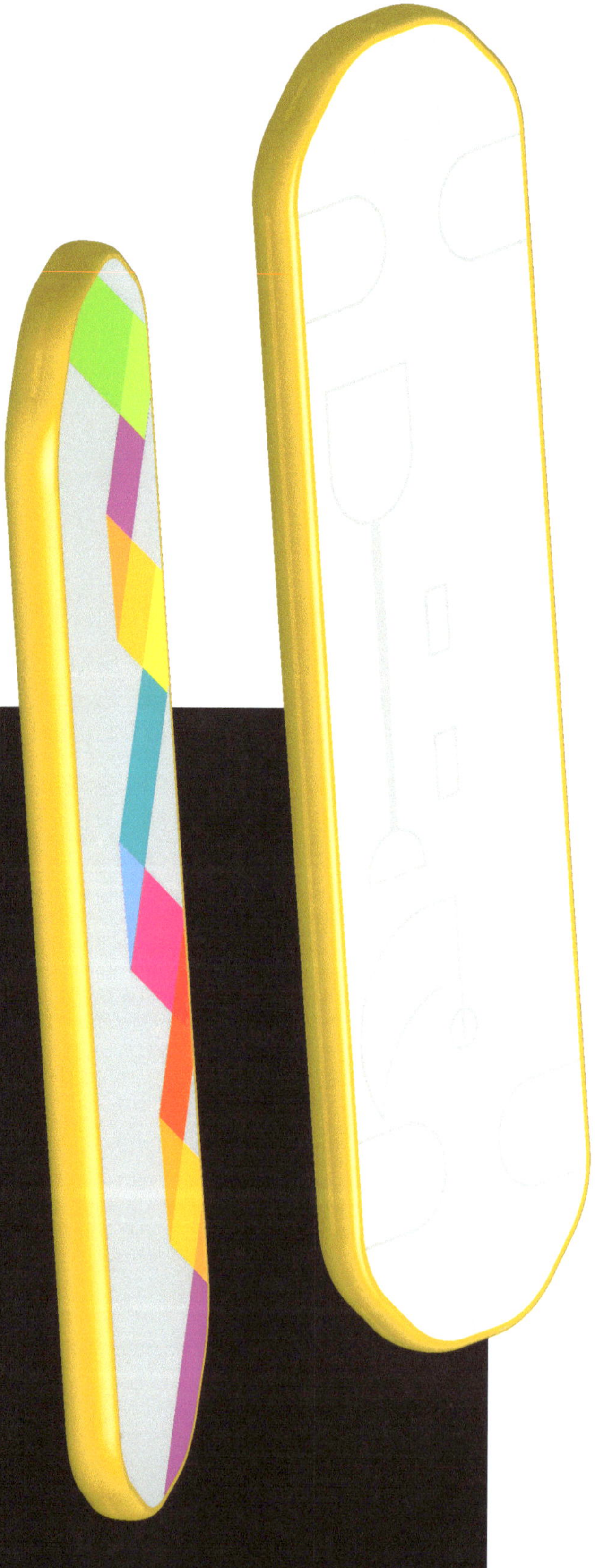

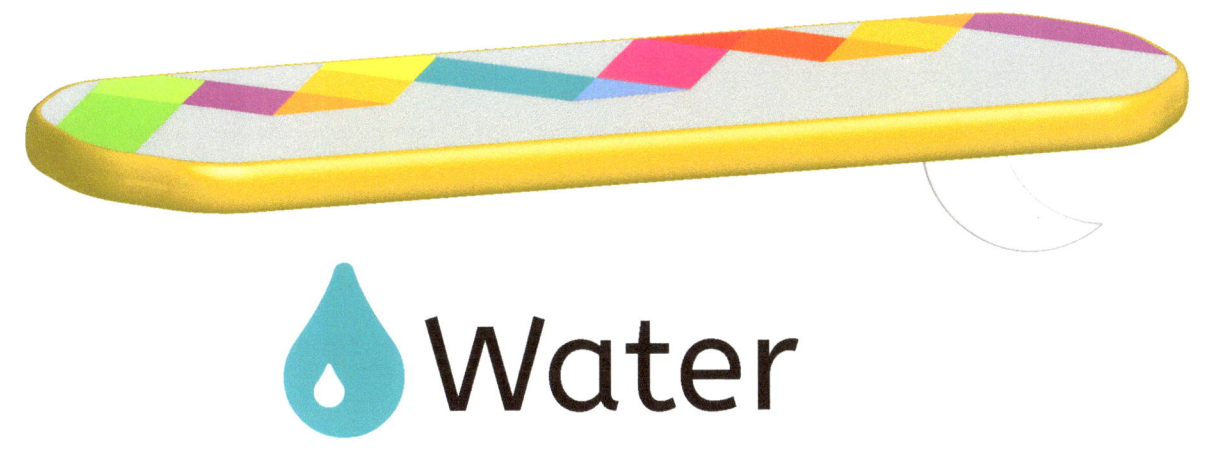
Water

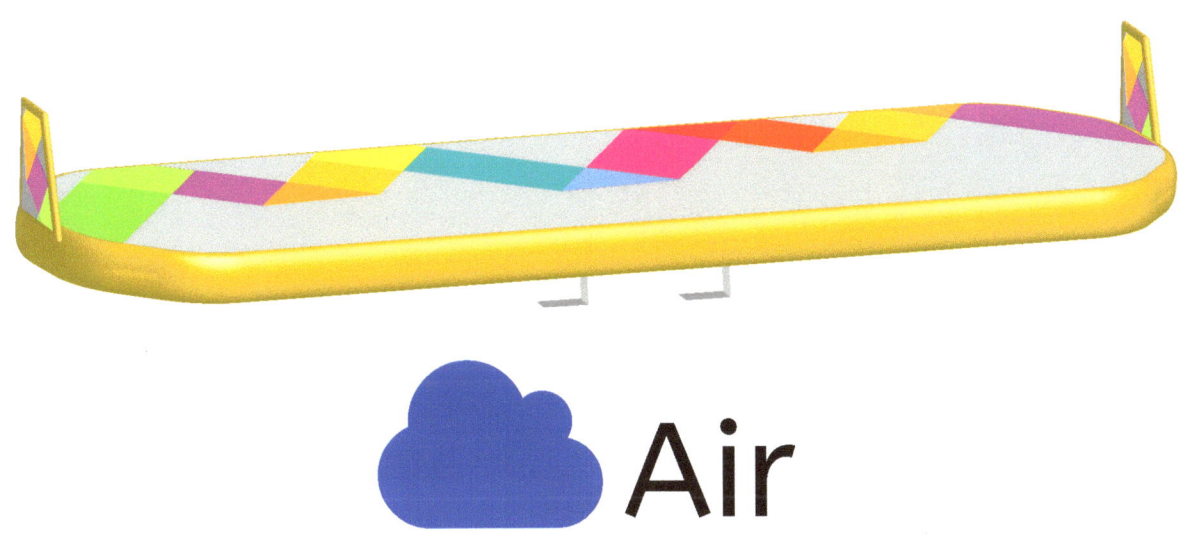
Air

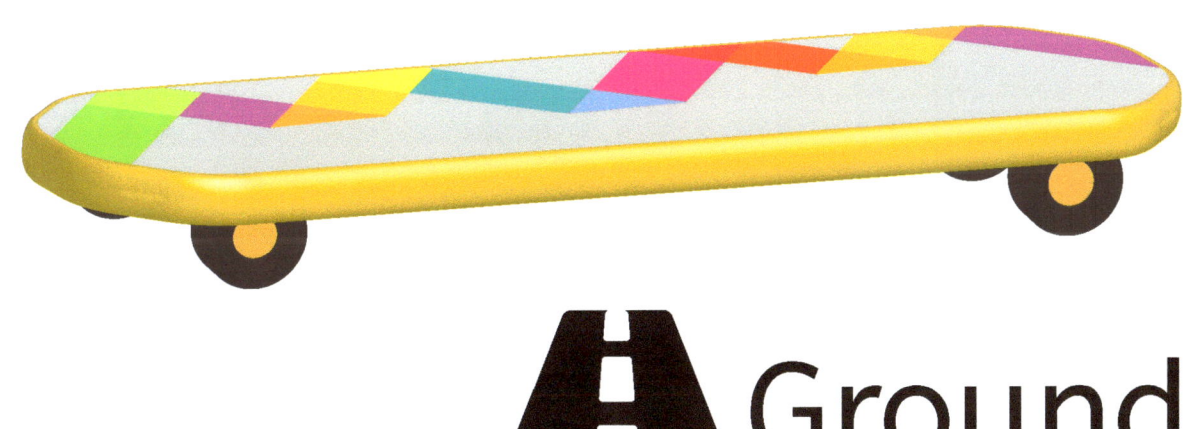
Ground

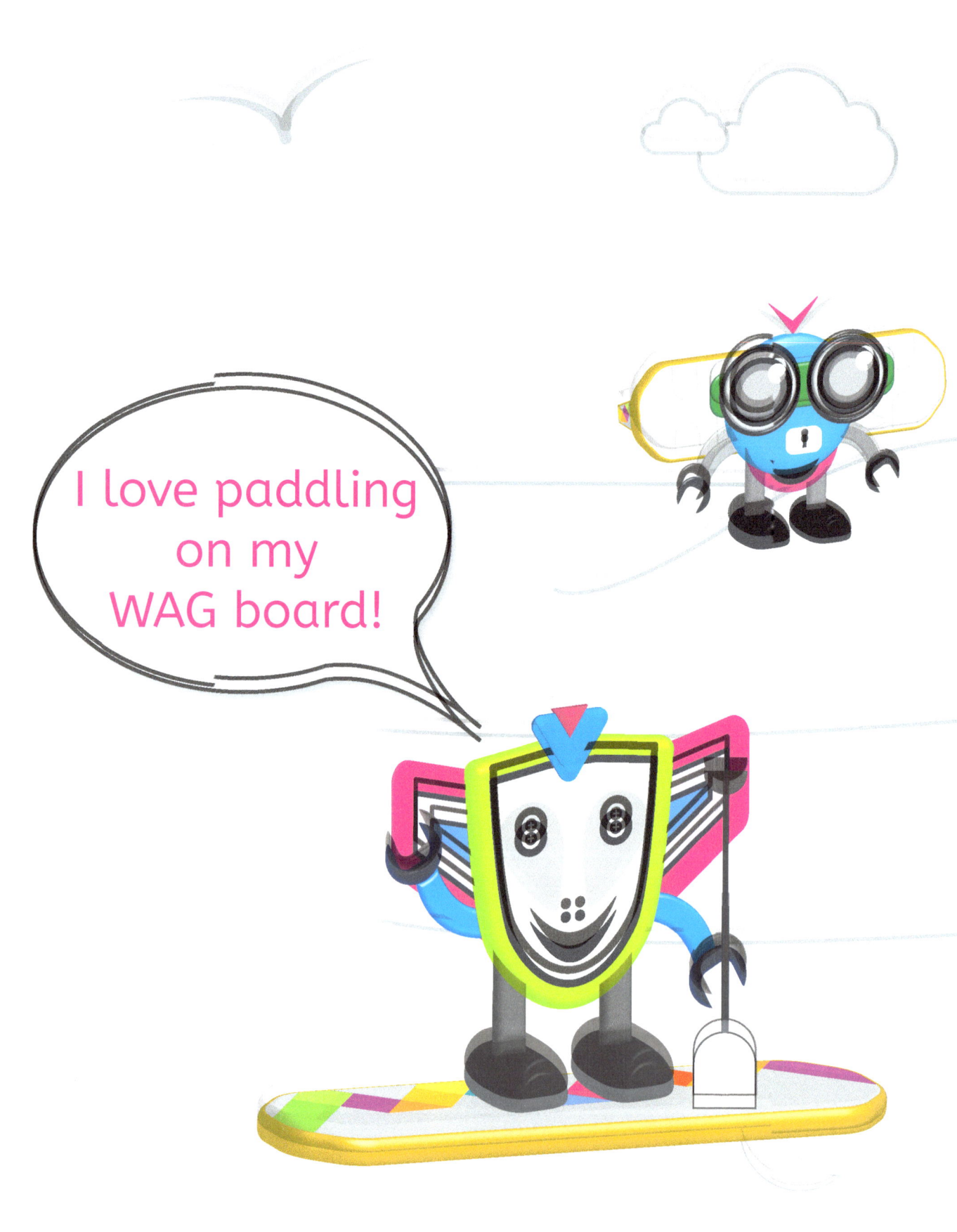

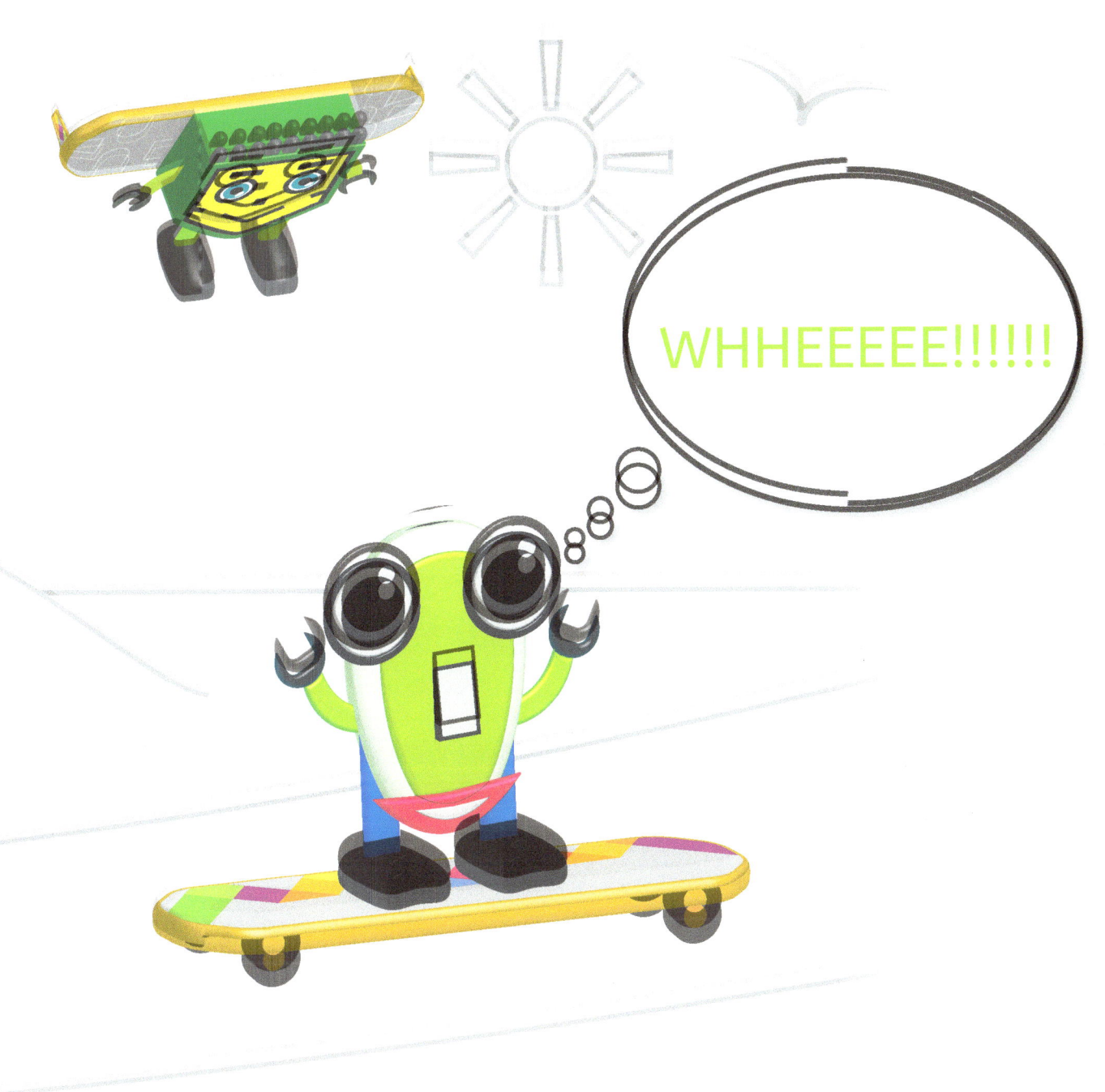

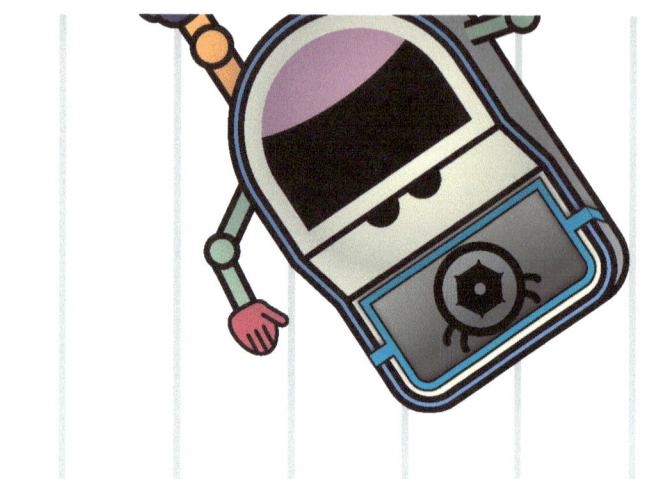
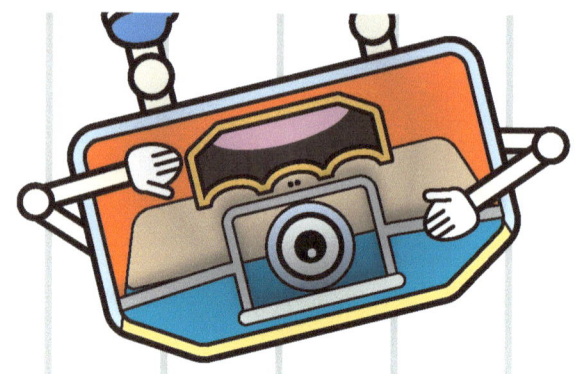
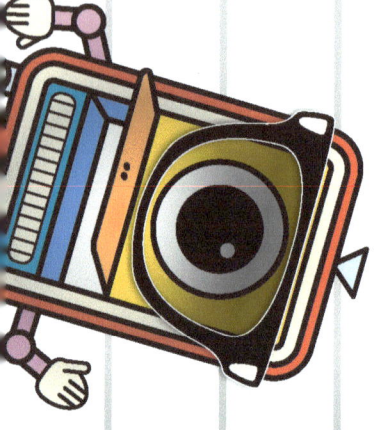
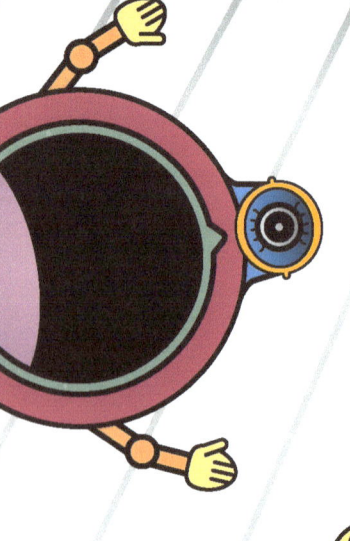
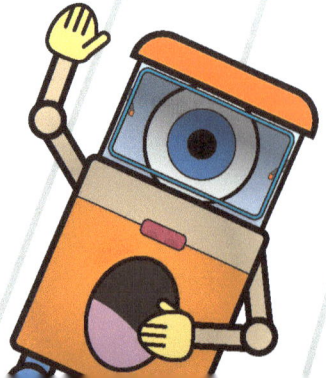
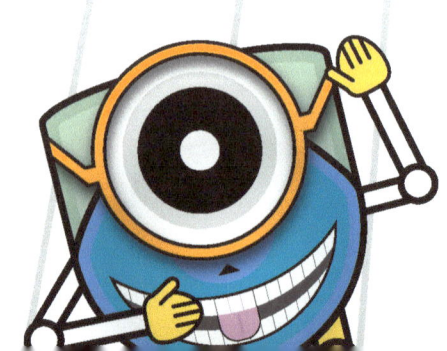

These Cyclops were hiding all around us.

Each character was discovered and created from a cycloptic face found in an everyday object.

How many more of these little characters are hiding around us?

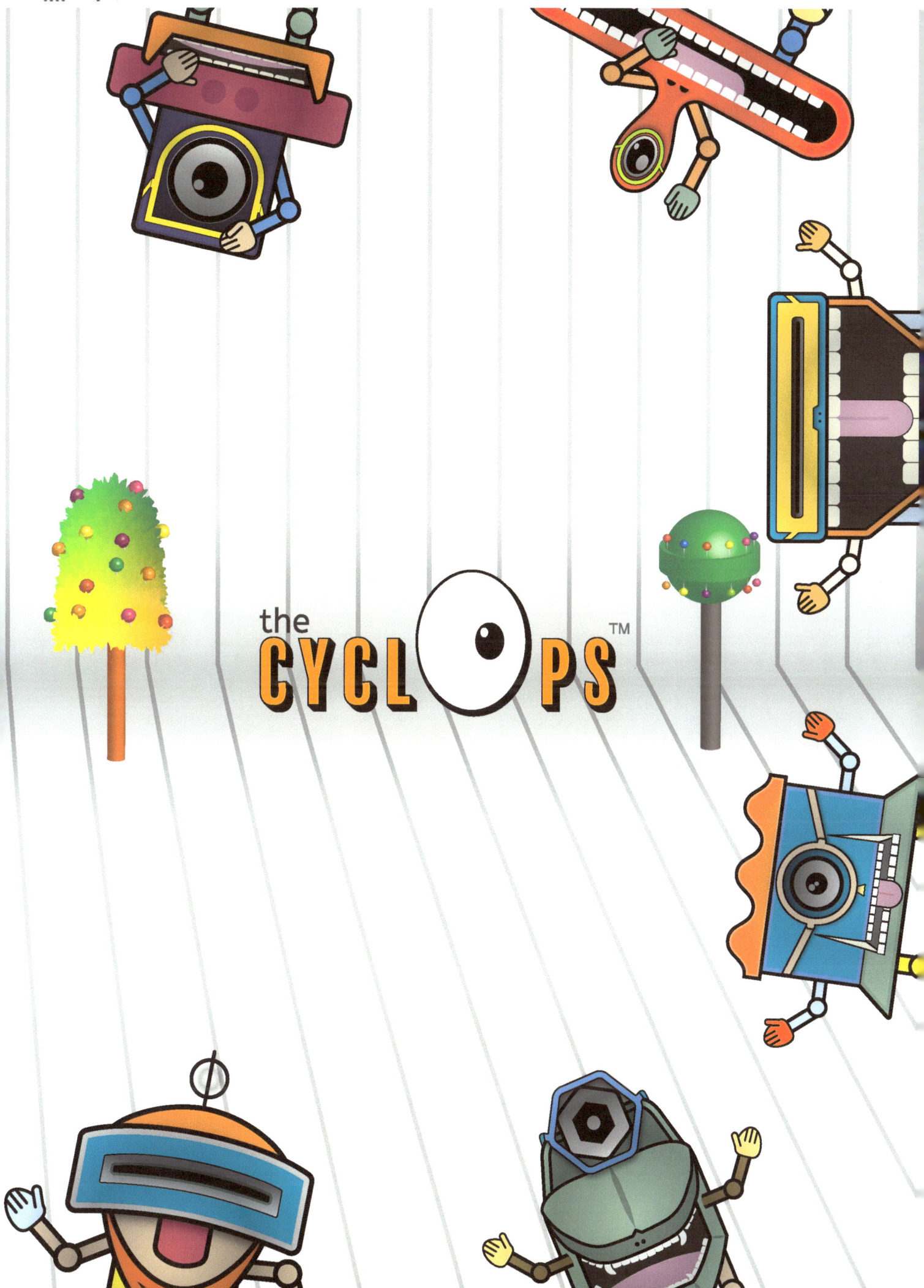

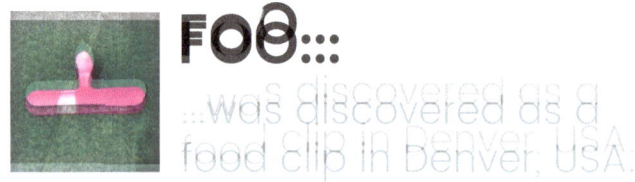

FOO...
...was discovered as a
food clip in Denver, USA.

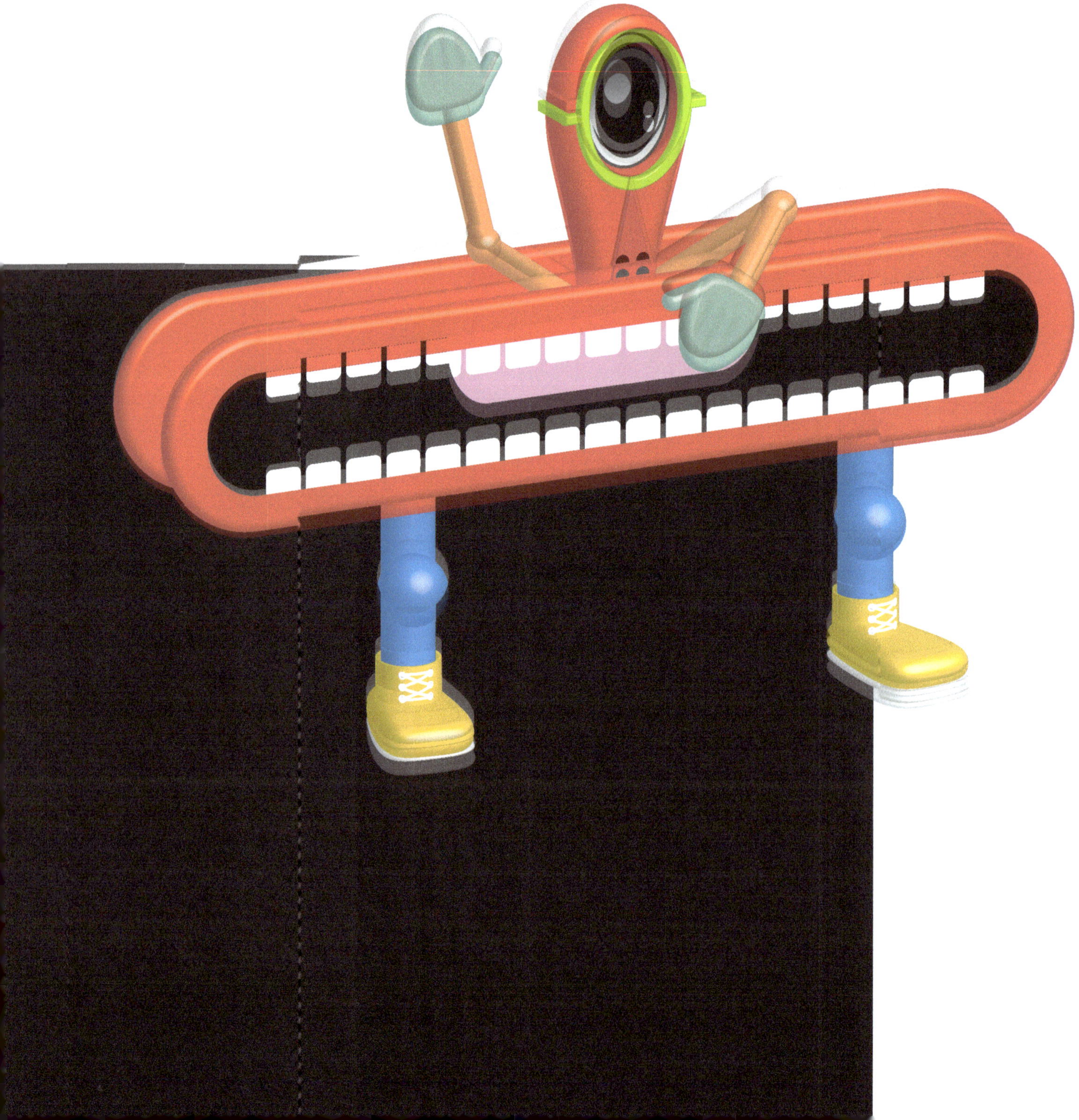

Reason for name:
From the first three letters of the word 'Food', Foo is the name of this little character.

Foo's Character:
Intelligent with fantastic intuition, Foo grasps new ideas and situations very quickly. Foo loves talking and is interested in many different topics.

Foo's Superpower:
Sharing the importance of the balance between the brain, heart and gut.

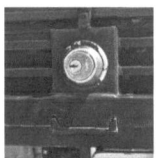

VIS...
...was hiding as a gate lock in San Francisco, USA.

Reason for name:
Vis' name was created from the first three letters of the word written on the lock that inspired this character. That word was 'Visalock'.

Vis' Character:
A trusted friend who is brilliant at keeping secrets, Vis helps everyone to feel secure.

Vis' Superpower:
With a strength of purpose as well as being physically strong, Vis supports and protects the other Cyclops.

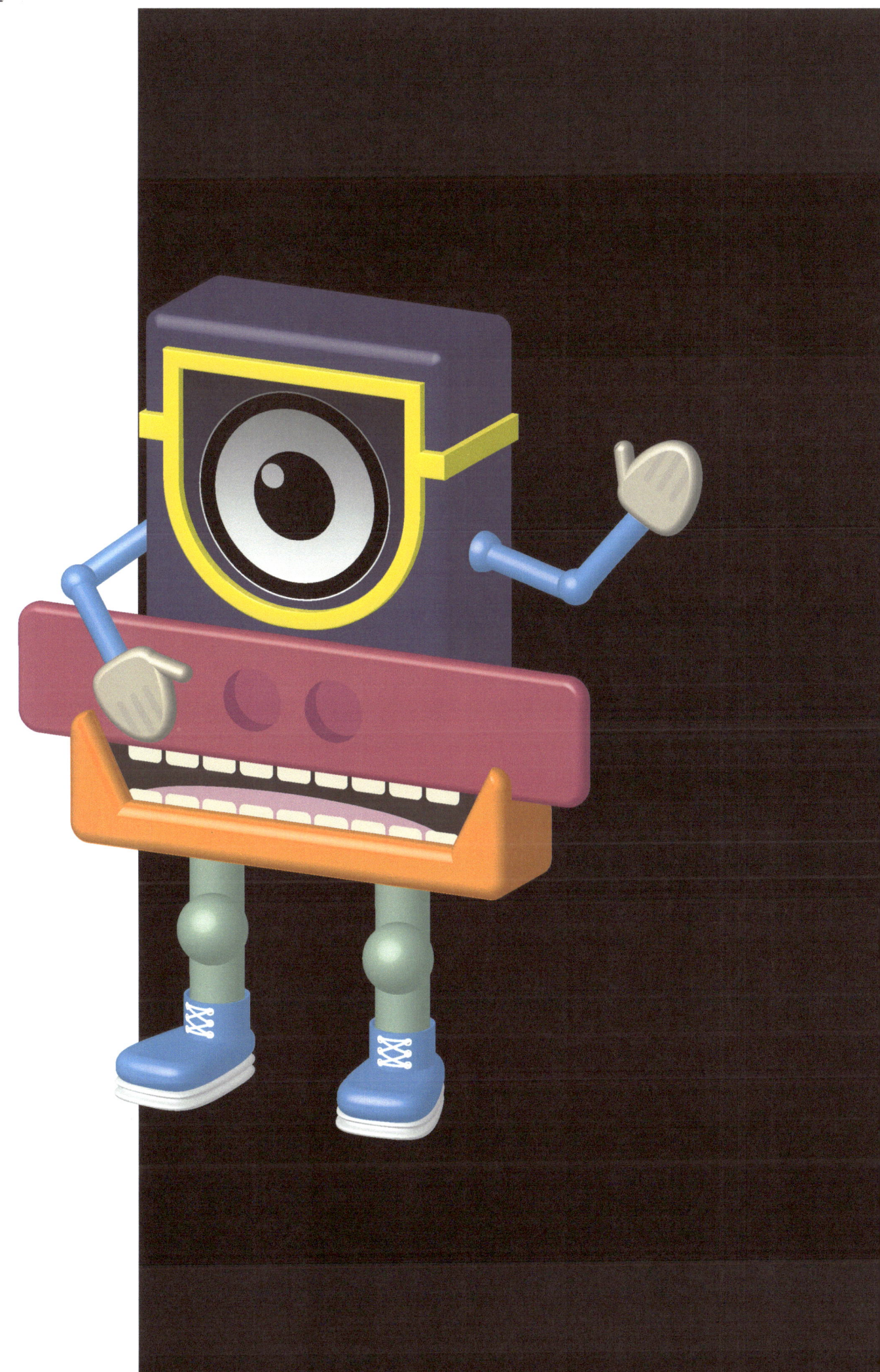

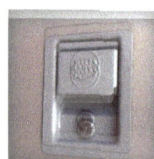 **HAN:::**
...was discovered as a handle on the side of a horsebox in Boulder, USA.

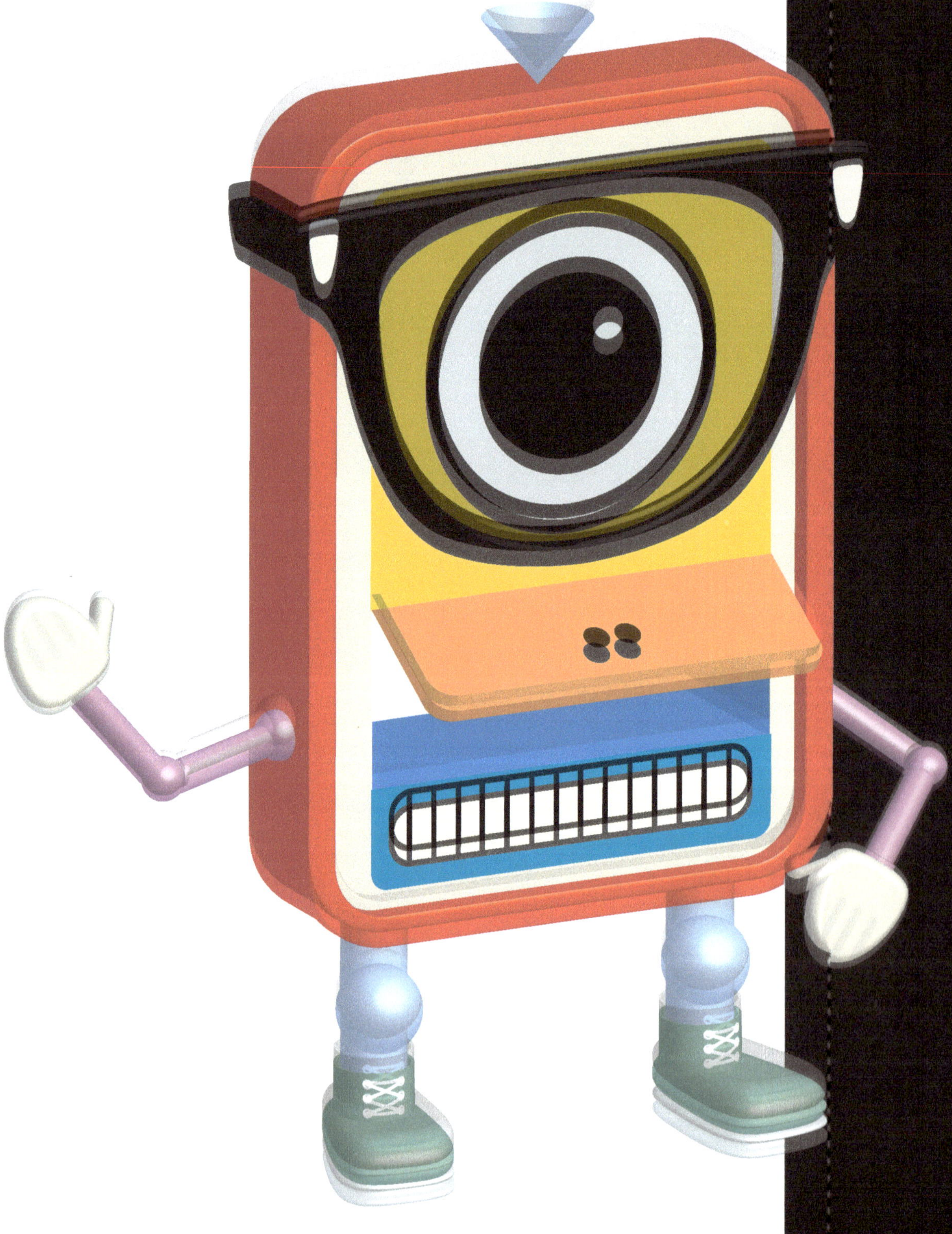

Reason for name:
Using the first three letters from the word Handle, Han is the name of this character.

Han's Character:
Loving to learn new things from factual books, Han is an introvert who loves reading.

Han's Superpower:
Helping give context to life and situations by referencing back to interesting and useful information found in books.

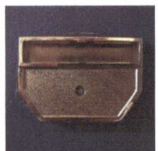 # LOC...

...was found as a hotel door lock in San Jose, USA.

Reason for name:
Using the first three letters from the word 'Lock', Loc is the name of this character.

Loc's Character:
Loud and brash, Loc loves to be the life and soul of the party. With an outgoing personality, Loc loves to be around others.

Loc's Superpower:
Empathetic and friendly, Loc is amazing at making new friends.

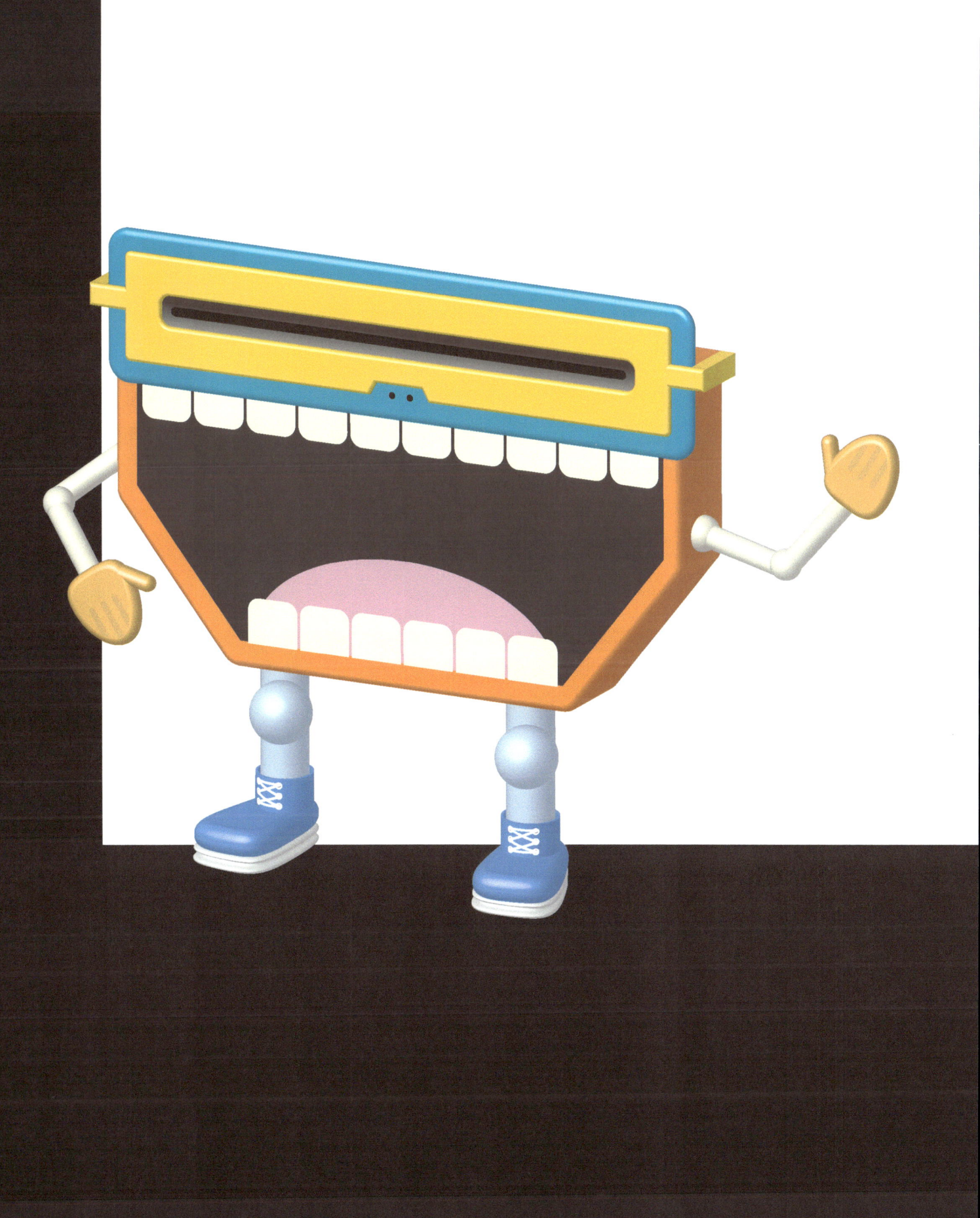

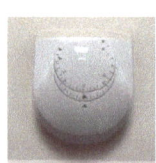

ERM:::
...was discovered as a thermostat on a wall in Frome, UK.

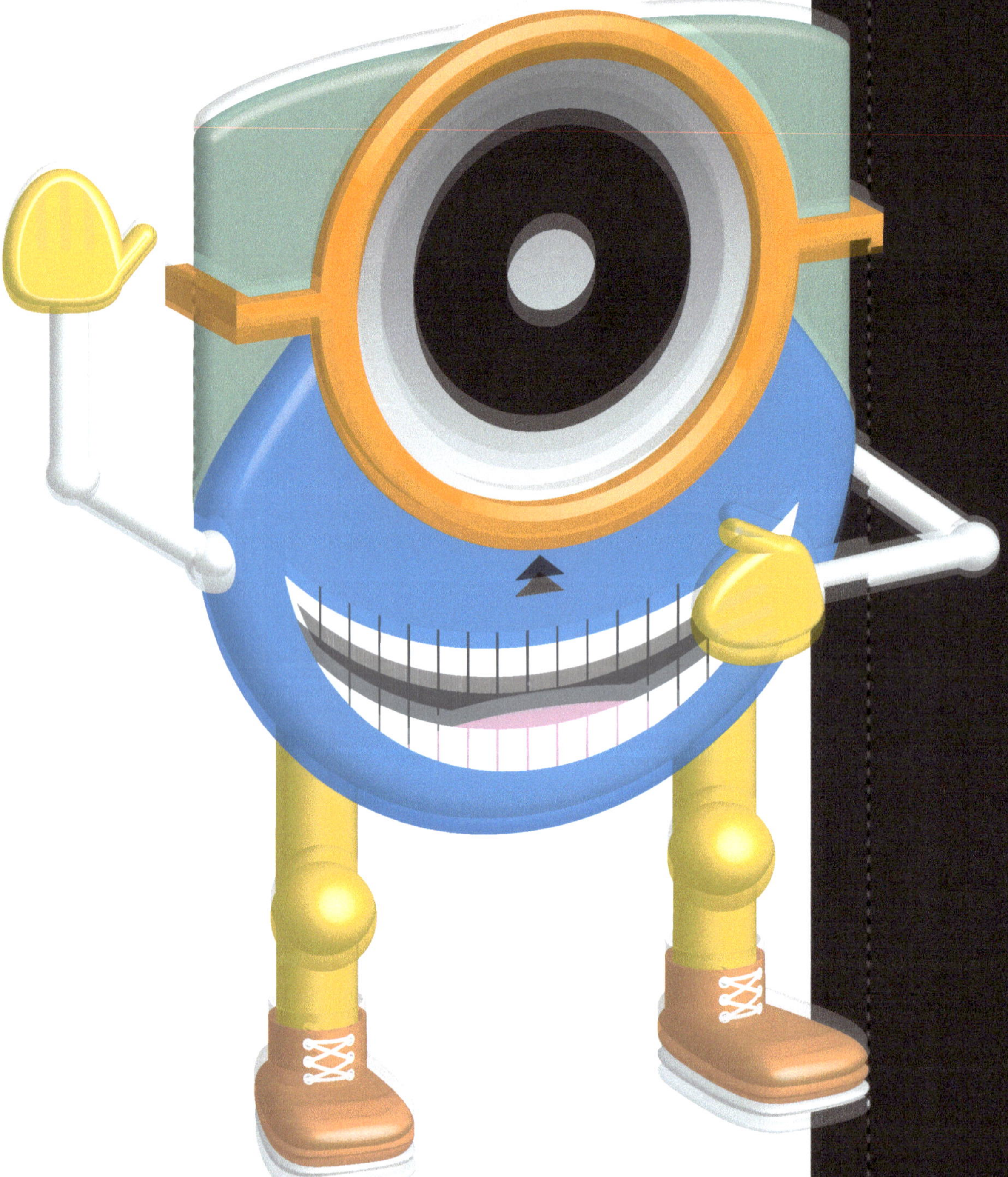

Reason for name:
Erm's name comes from the third, fourth and fifth letters of the word 'Thermostat'.

Erm's Character:
With a warm heart and a positive outlook on life, Erm loves lifting others when they are feeling down. With the ability to see every side of a situation, Erm can get confused about what to do next, resulting in analysis paralysis.

Erm's Superpower:
Being emotionally rather than intellectually led, Erm is very good at recognising how events and situations may make others feel.

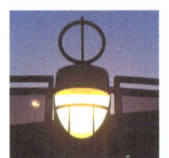 **LIG...**
...was discovered as a light on a pillar in Osaka, Japan.

Reason for name:
Taking the first three letters from the word 'Light', Lig is the name of this character.

Lig's Character:
Bright and breezy, Lig is very relaxed and goes with the flow of life. Fantastic at guiding, Lig is always there to help shine a light on any possible solutions.

Lig's Superpower:
Being supportive and creative, Lig loves to help others to explore their options.

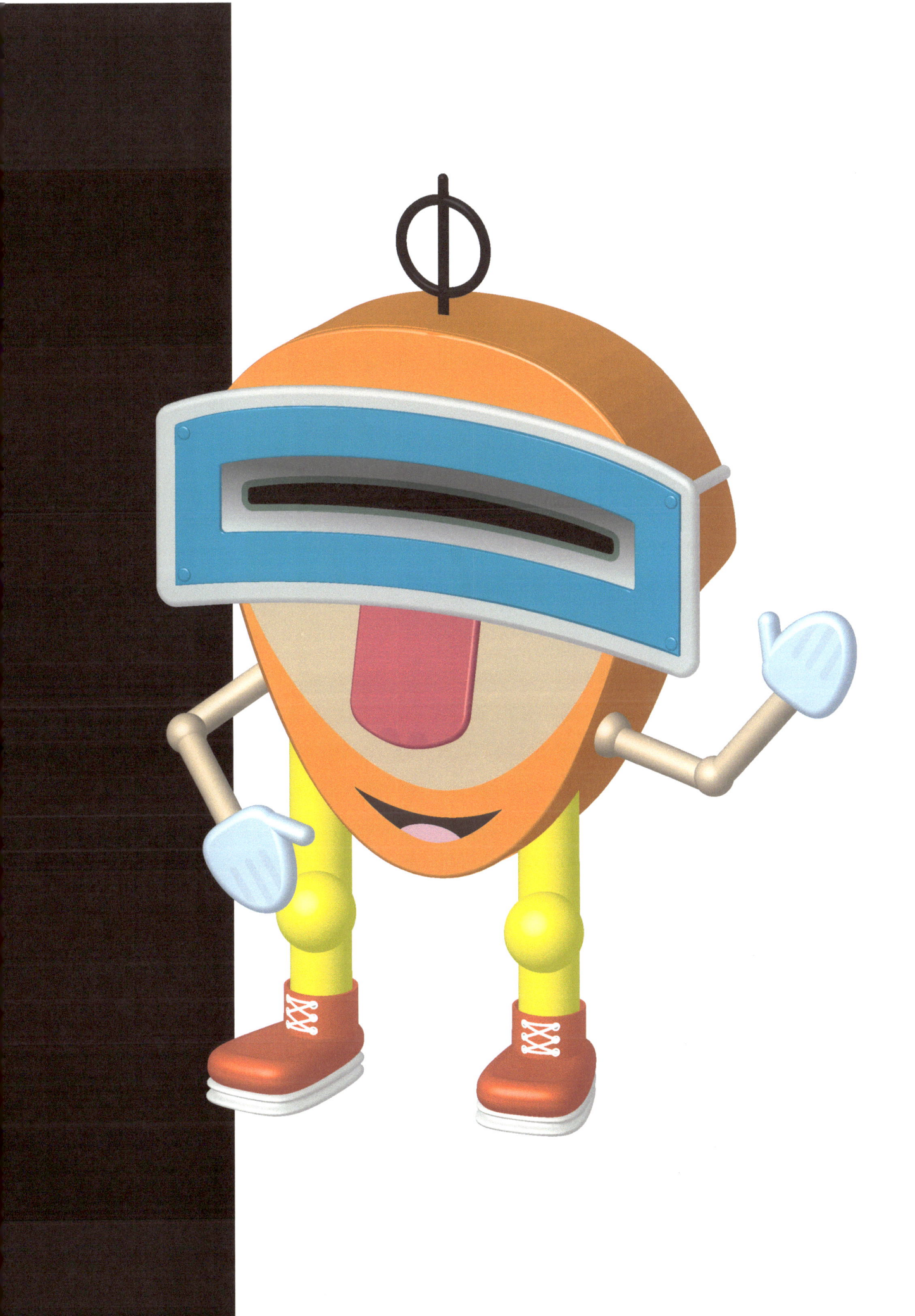

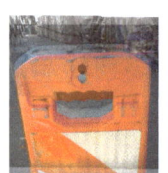 **RAF:::**
...was found as a traffic cone in Denver, USA:

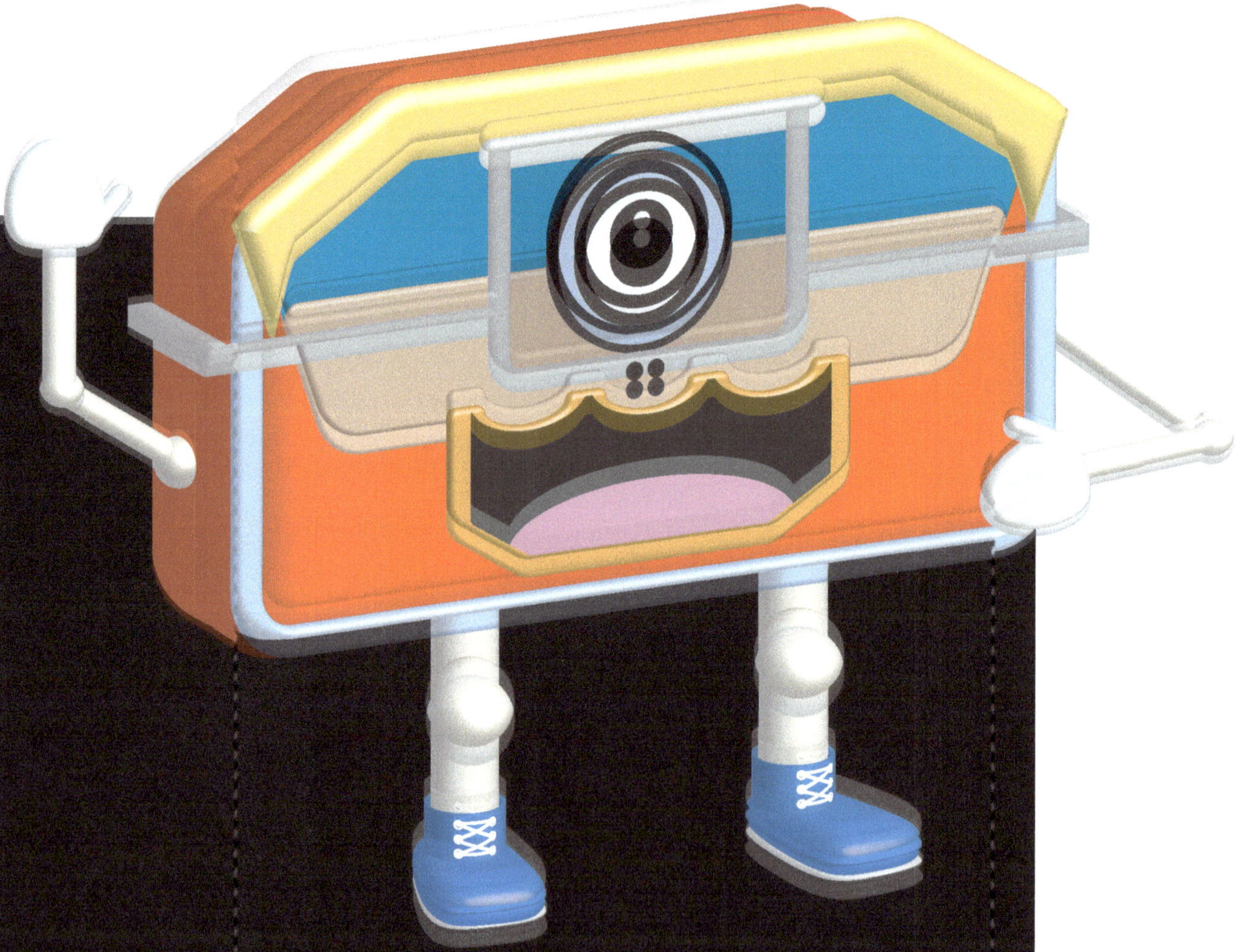

Reason for name:
Raf's name comes from the second, third and fourth letters from the word 'Traffic Cone'.

Raf's Character:
Always balanced, with a bright and vibrant personality, Raf is a joy to be around.

Raf's Superpower:
Having lived a full and interesting life, Raf's superpower of experience and wisdom keeps everyone safe.

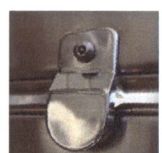 # STO...
...was discovered as a toilet door stop in Chicago, USA

Reason for name:
Taking the first three letters from the word 'Stop', Sto is the name of this character.

Sto's Character:
Slow and steady, Sto is very considered in every activity and appreciates each and every moment.

Sto's Superpower:
Being able to meditate and relax, Sto helps the other Cyclops to slow down and think before acting.

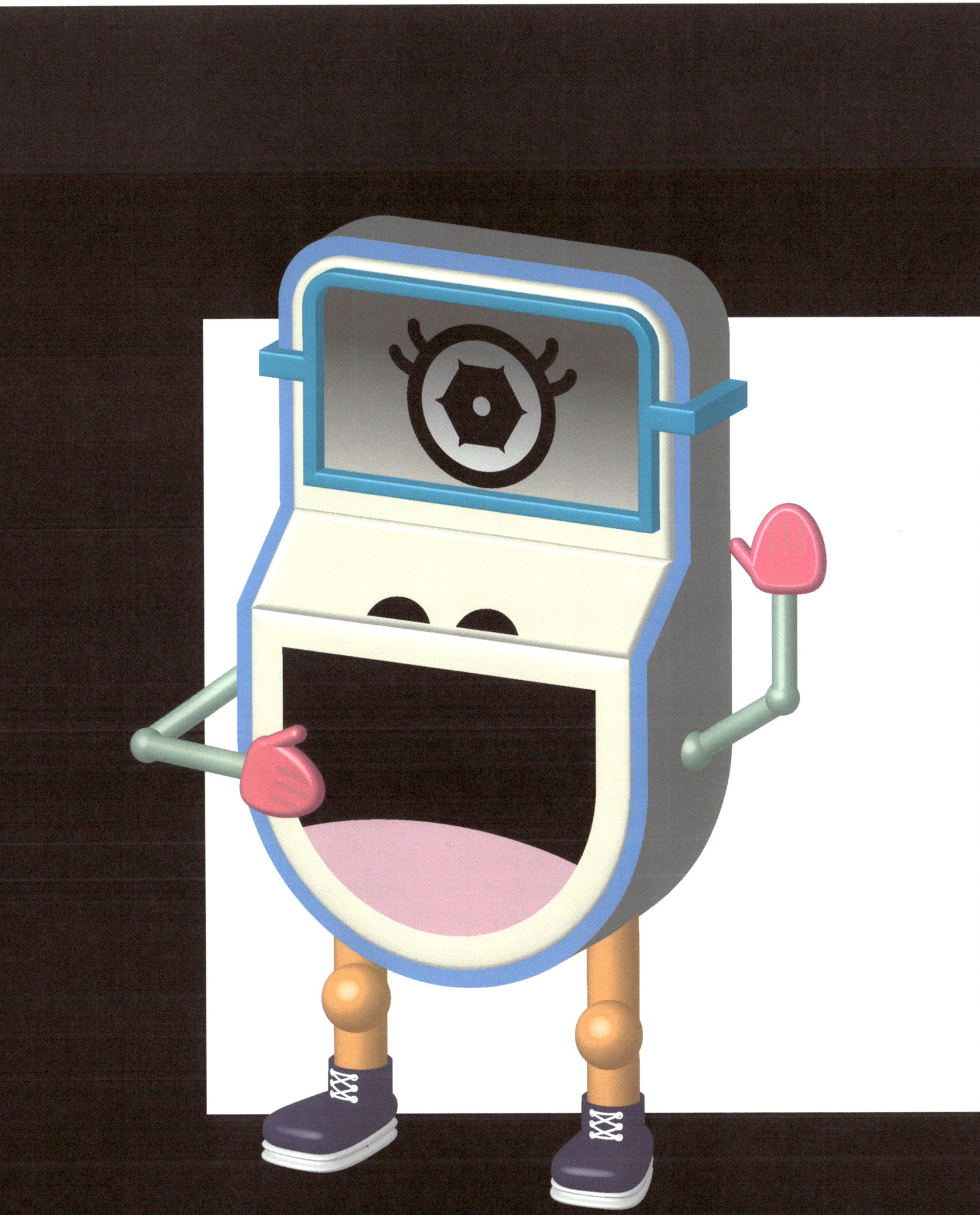

SEN:::

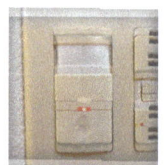

...was discovered in San Jose, USA as a light sensor.

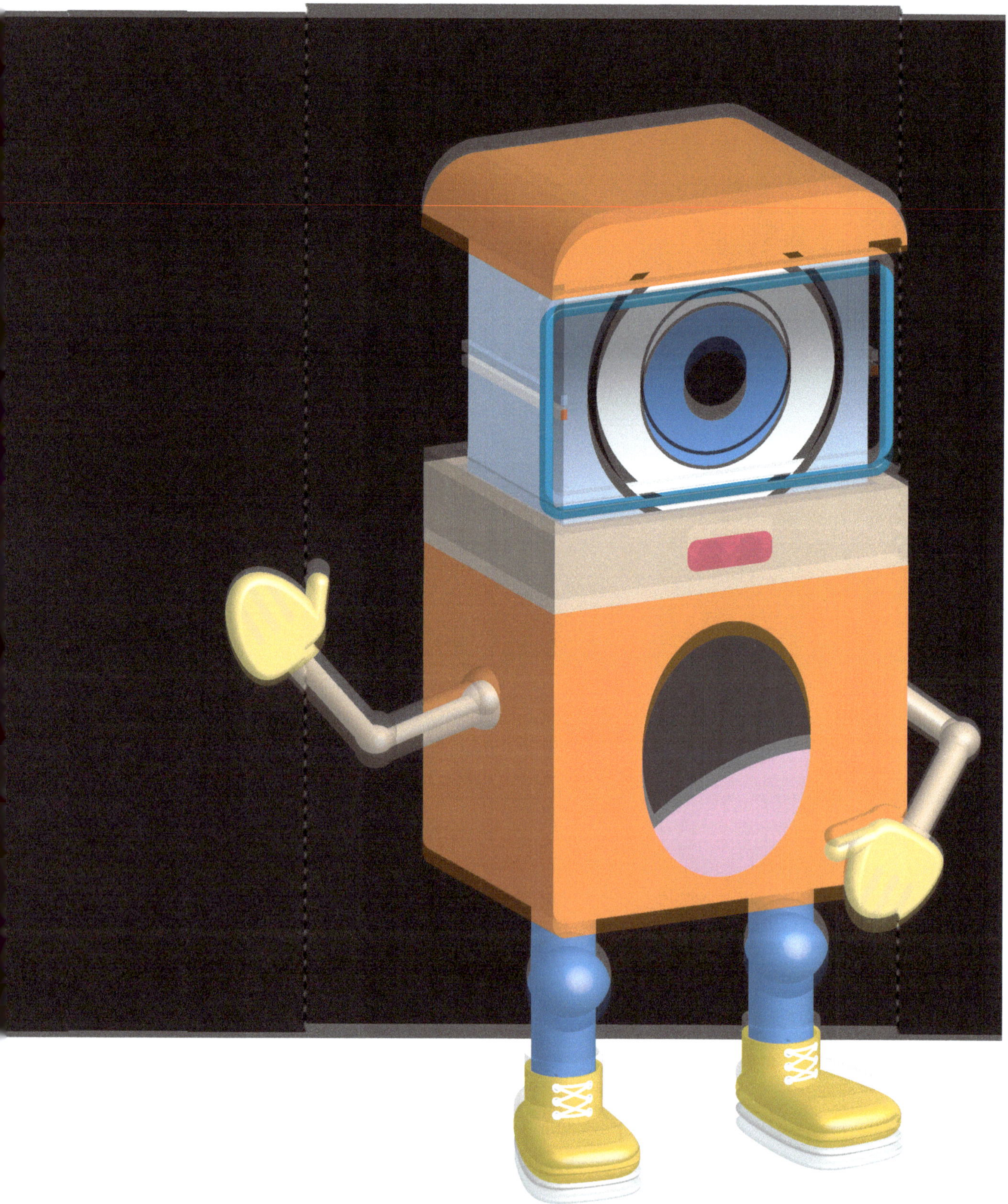

Reason for name:
From the first three letters of the word 'Sensor: Sen in the name of this character.

Sen's Character:
A hugger who loves to connect with others with the heart rather than through the mind. Sen is warm and caring with a fantastic gut instinct.

Sen's Superpower:
Sen is brilliant at sensing any changes in emotions, situations and even the weather.

RAI...

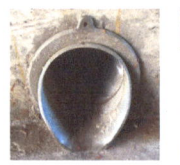

...was found as a drain pipe in Denver, USA.

Reason for name:
Rai's name comes from the second, third and fourth letters of the word 'Drain pipe'.

Rai's Character:
With a very relaxed demeanour, Rai is chilled and a delight to be around because nothing is too much trouble.

Rai's Superpower:
Going with the flow of life and never fighting reality.

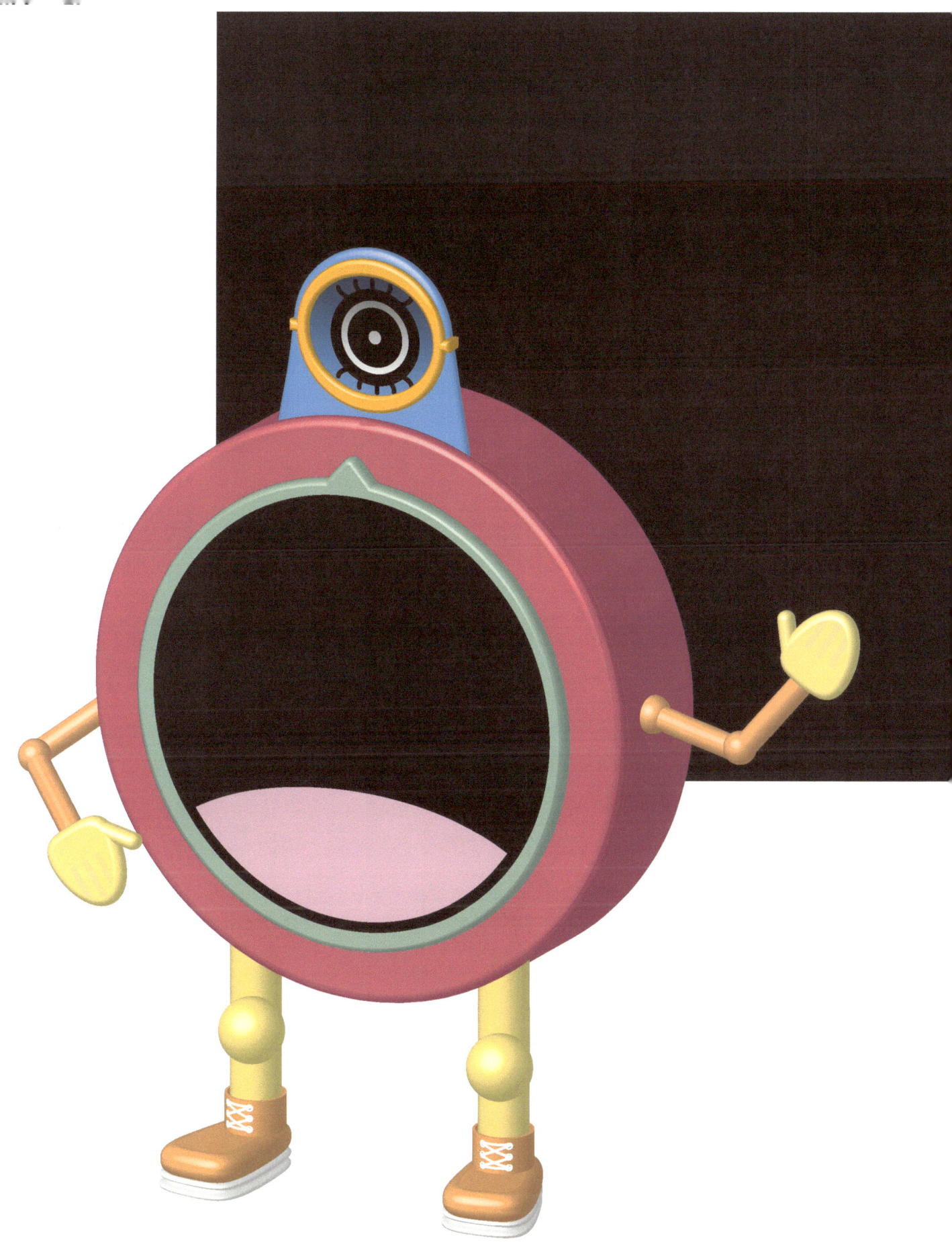

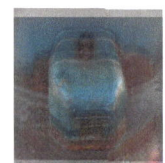 # POS:::
...was discovered at the bottom of a post in Denver, USA.

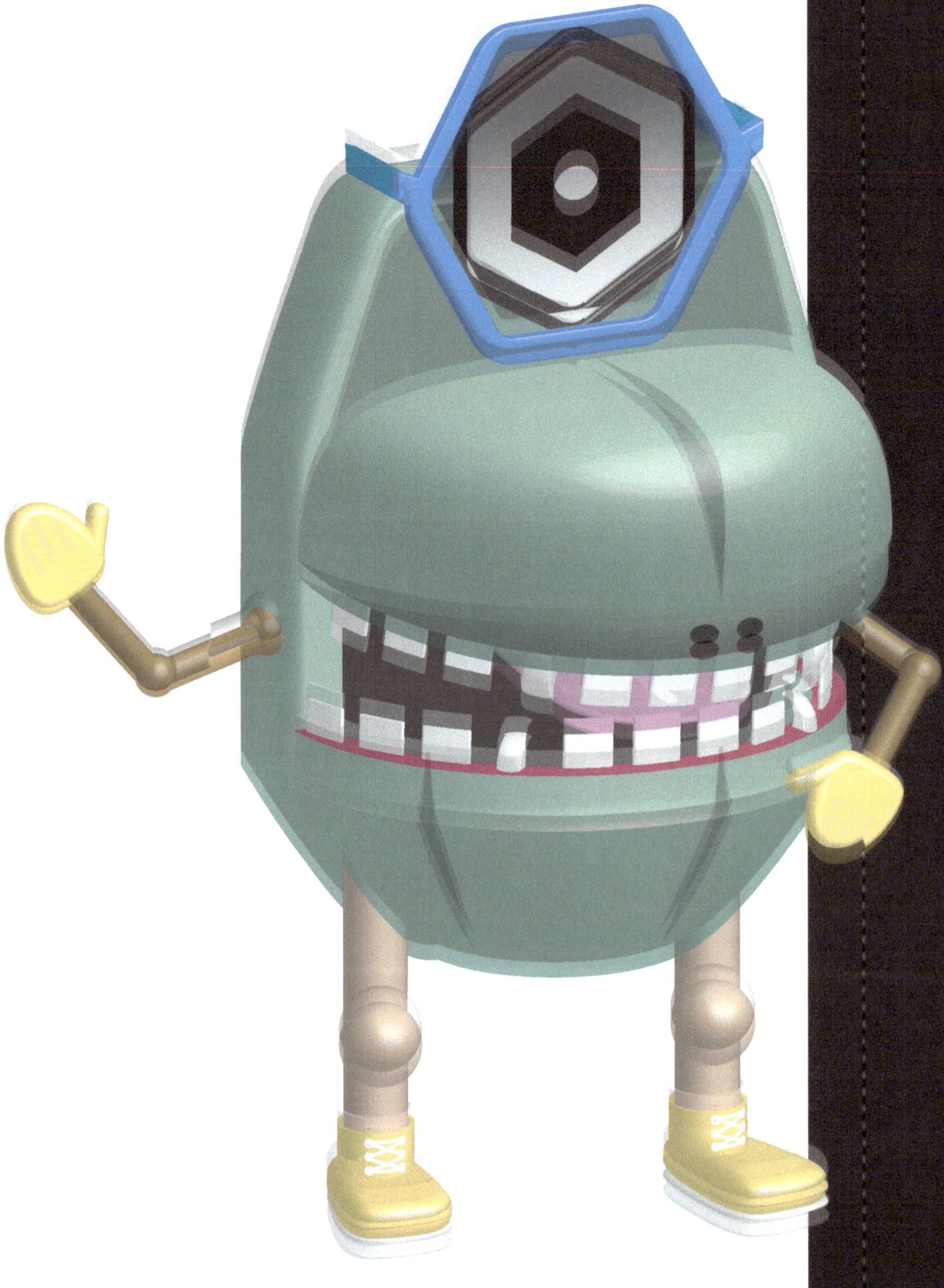

Reason for name:
Pos is named after the first three letters of the word 'Post'.

Pos' Character:
As a pillar of the community, Pos is supportive, balanced and a great shoulder to lean on in difficult times.

Pos' Superpower:
As a steady and reliable character, Pos' superpower is that of being caring and very supportive.

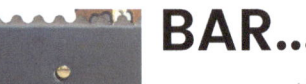

BAR...

...was discovered as a concrete barrier at the Pier in Santa Monica, USA.

Reason for name:
Bar is named after the first three letters of the word 'Barrier'.

Bar's Character:
Very caring to others, Bar loves to help everyone by being there when needed.

Bar's Superpower:
Being strong, steady and a rock that everyone can trust, Bar's superpower is helping others find their way by listening and being honest.

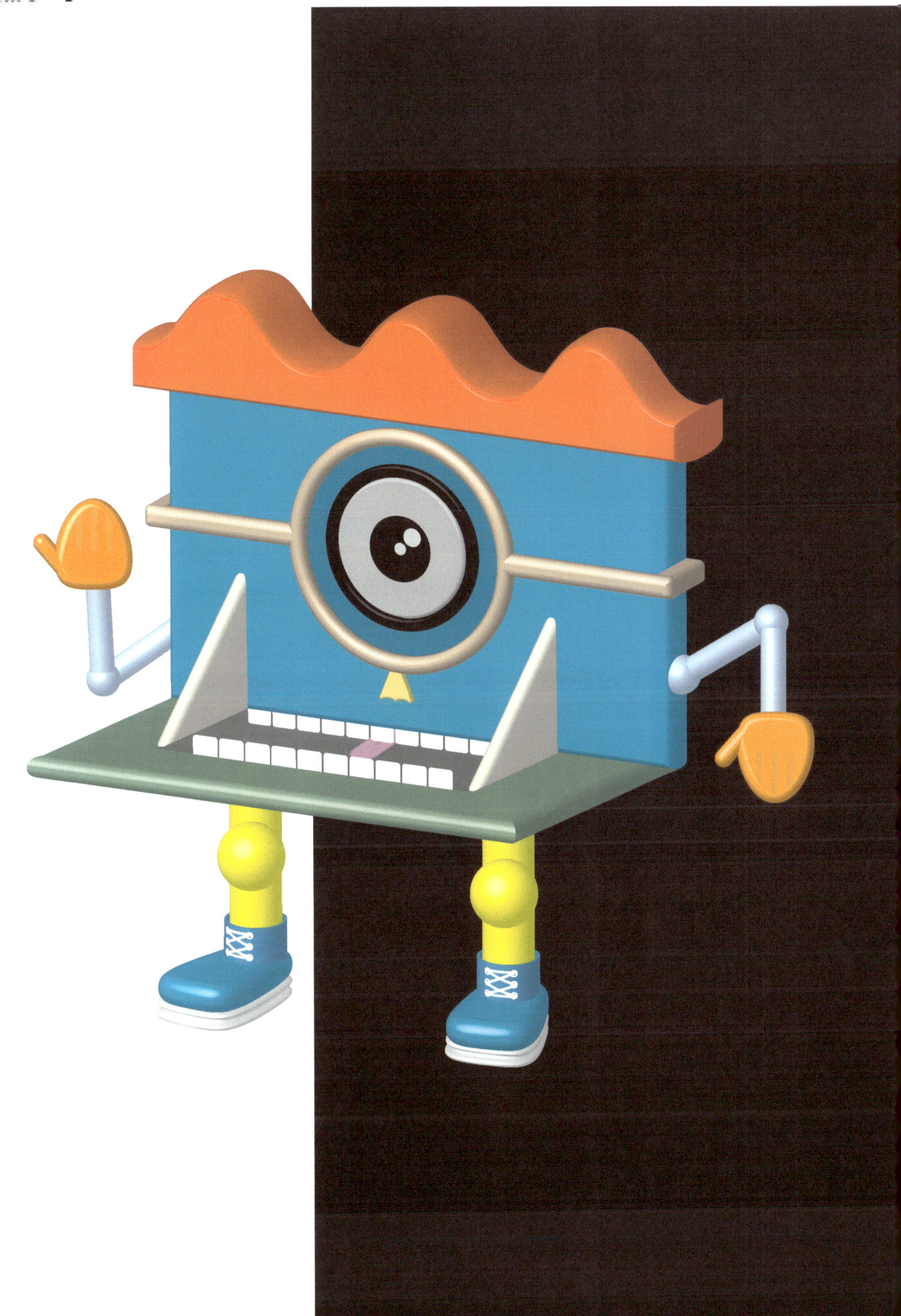

THE UNICLOPTER

The Cyclops travel along the ground and in the air on their Uniclopter.

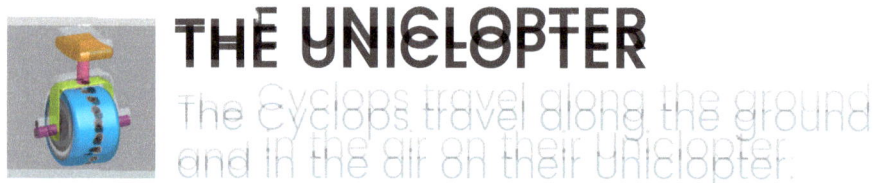

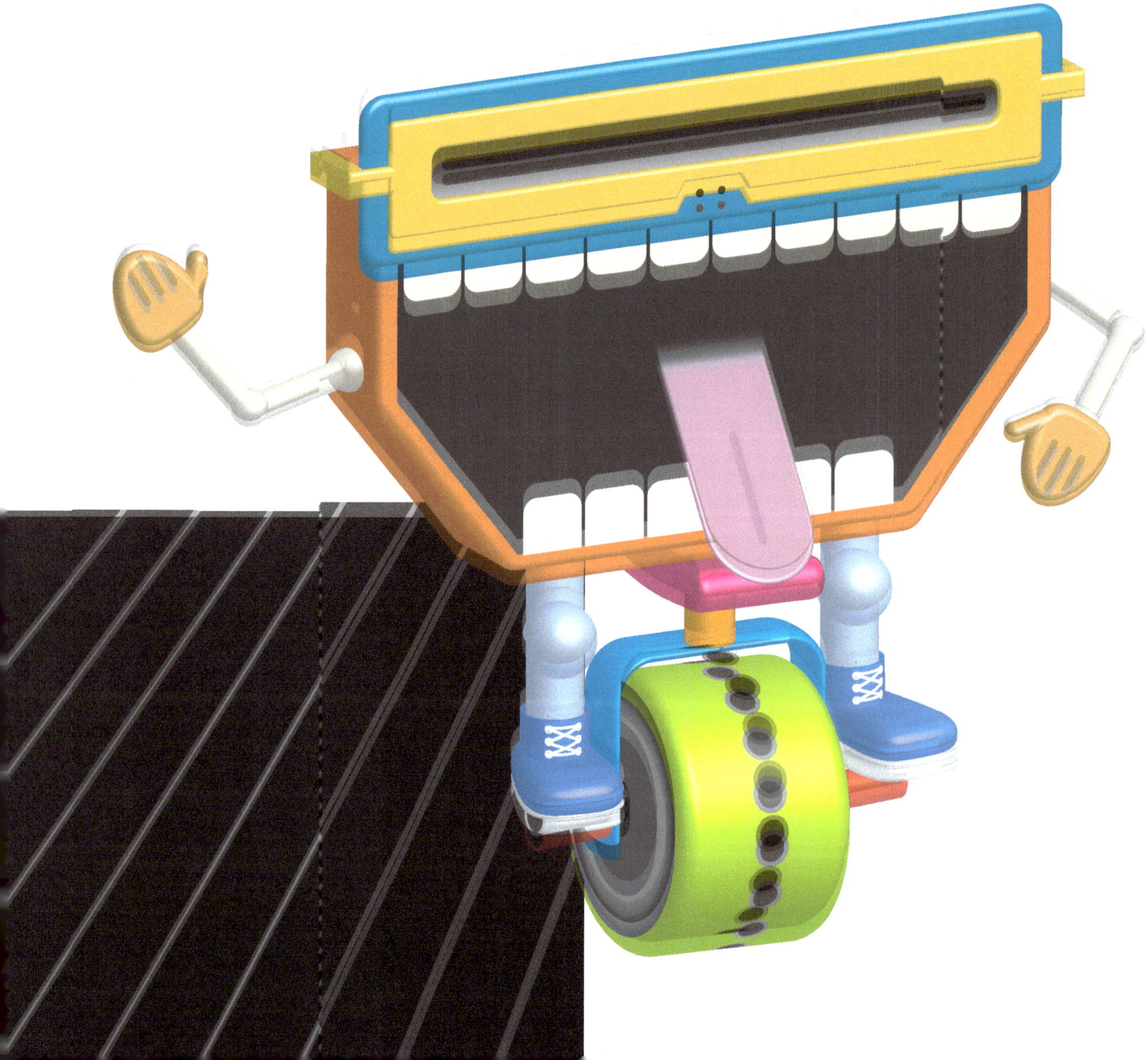

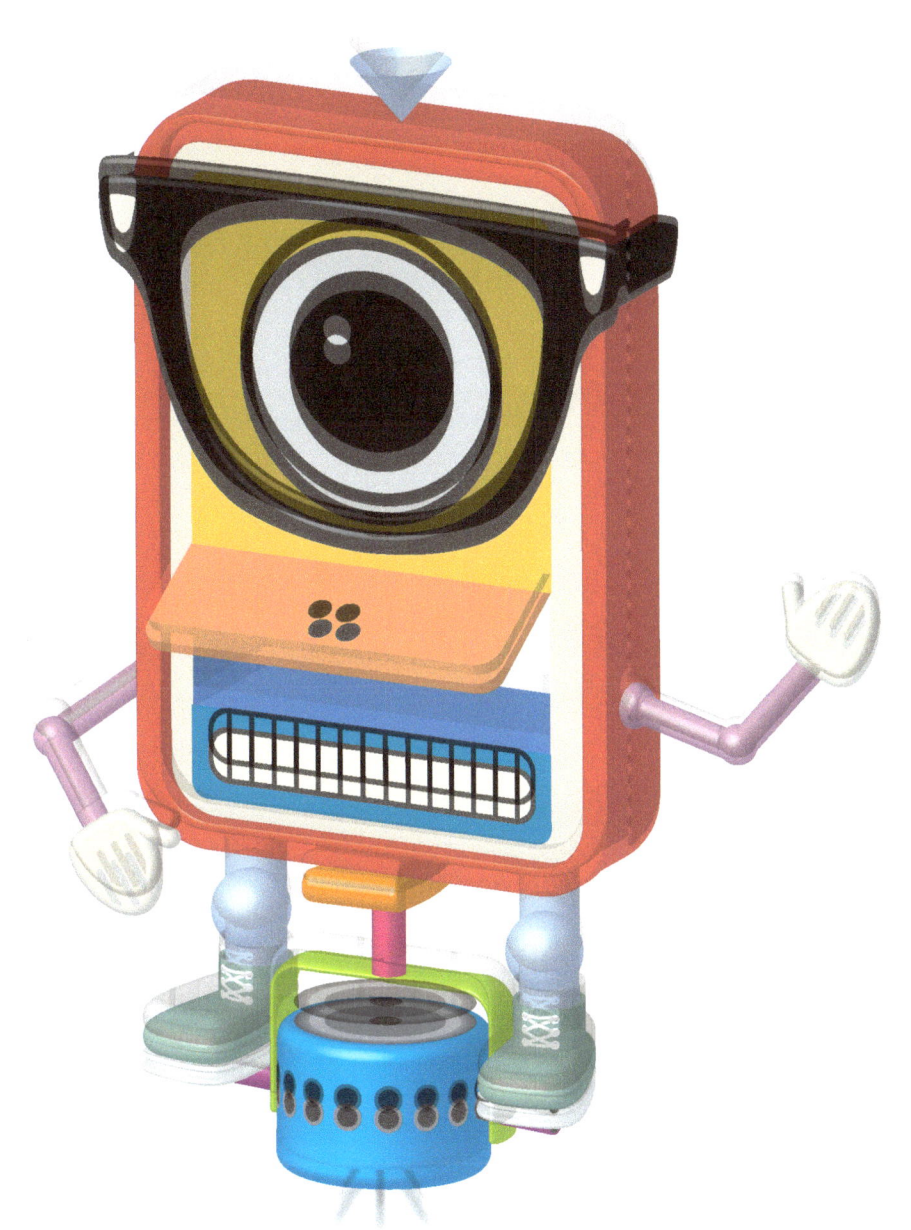

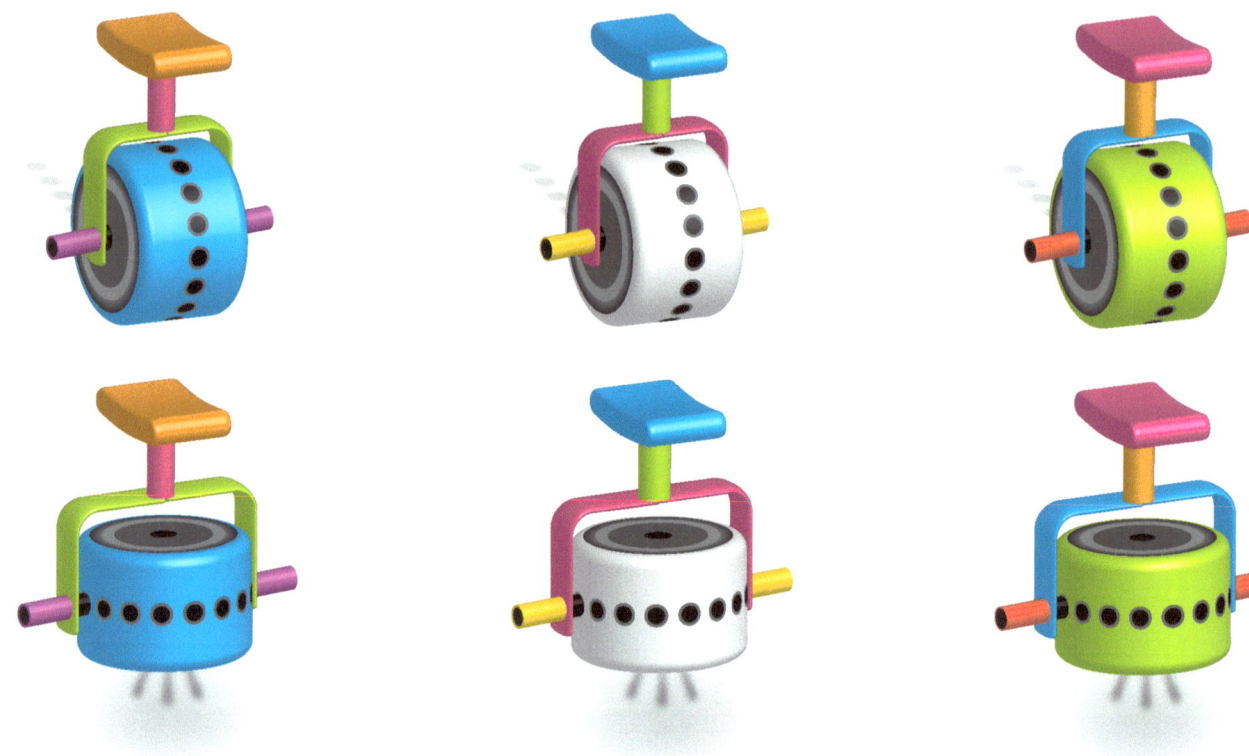

The Cyclop's

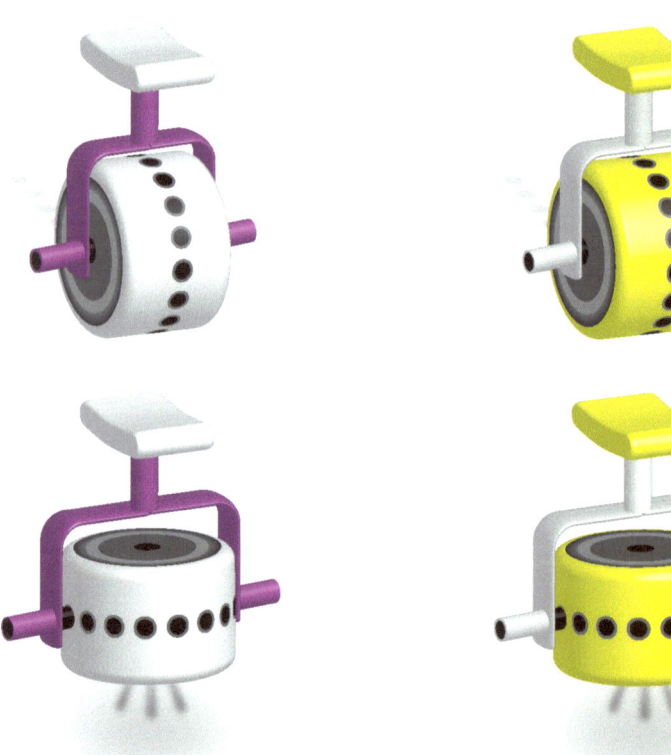
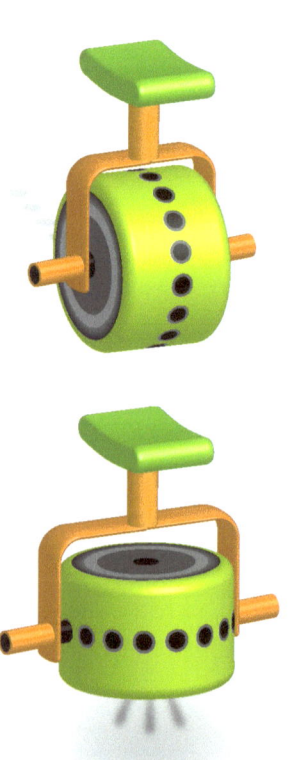

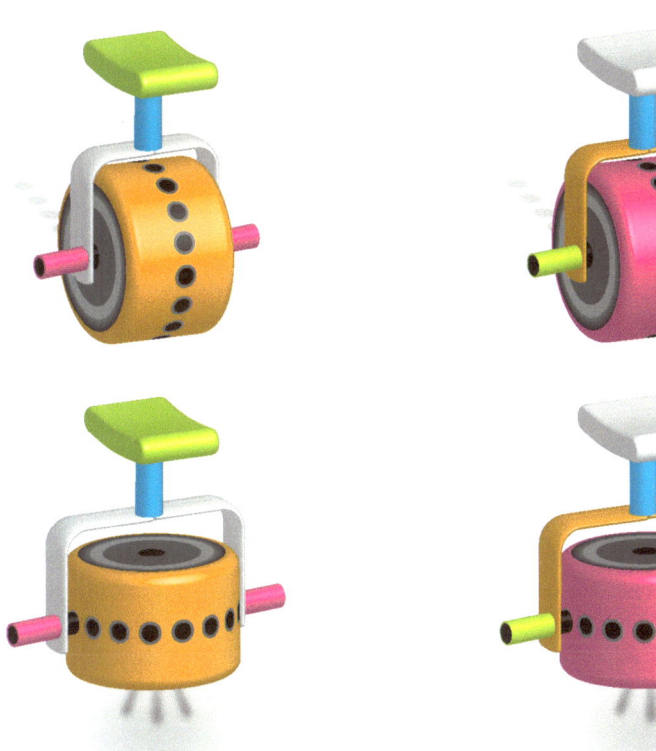
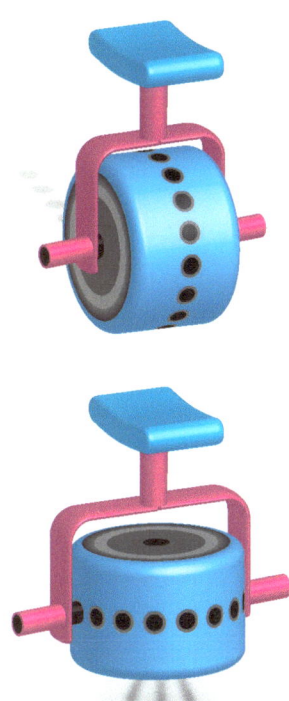

Uniclopter

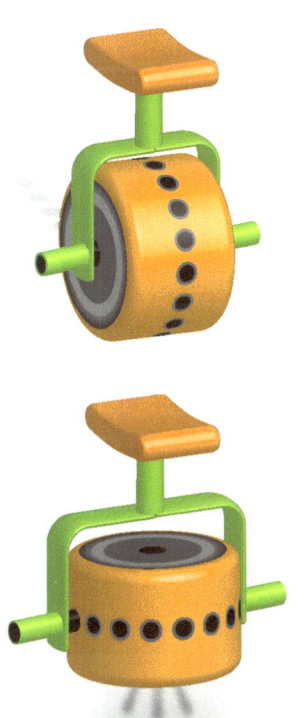
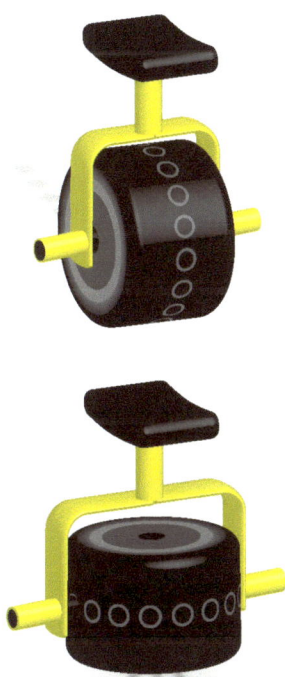
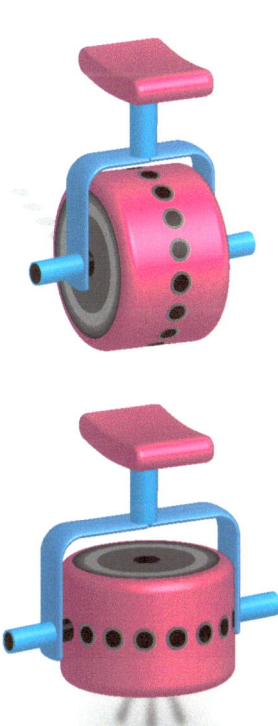

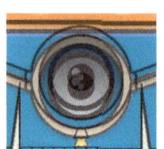 **ALL THE CYCLOP'S WEAR GLASSES...**
...that finds, sorts, zooms as well as changes the colour and shape of different objects.

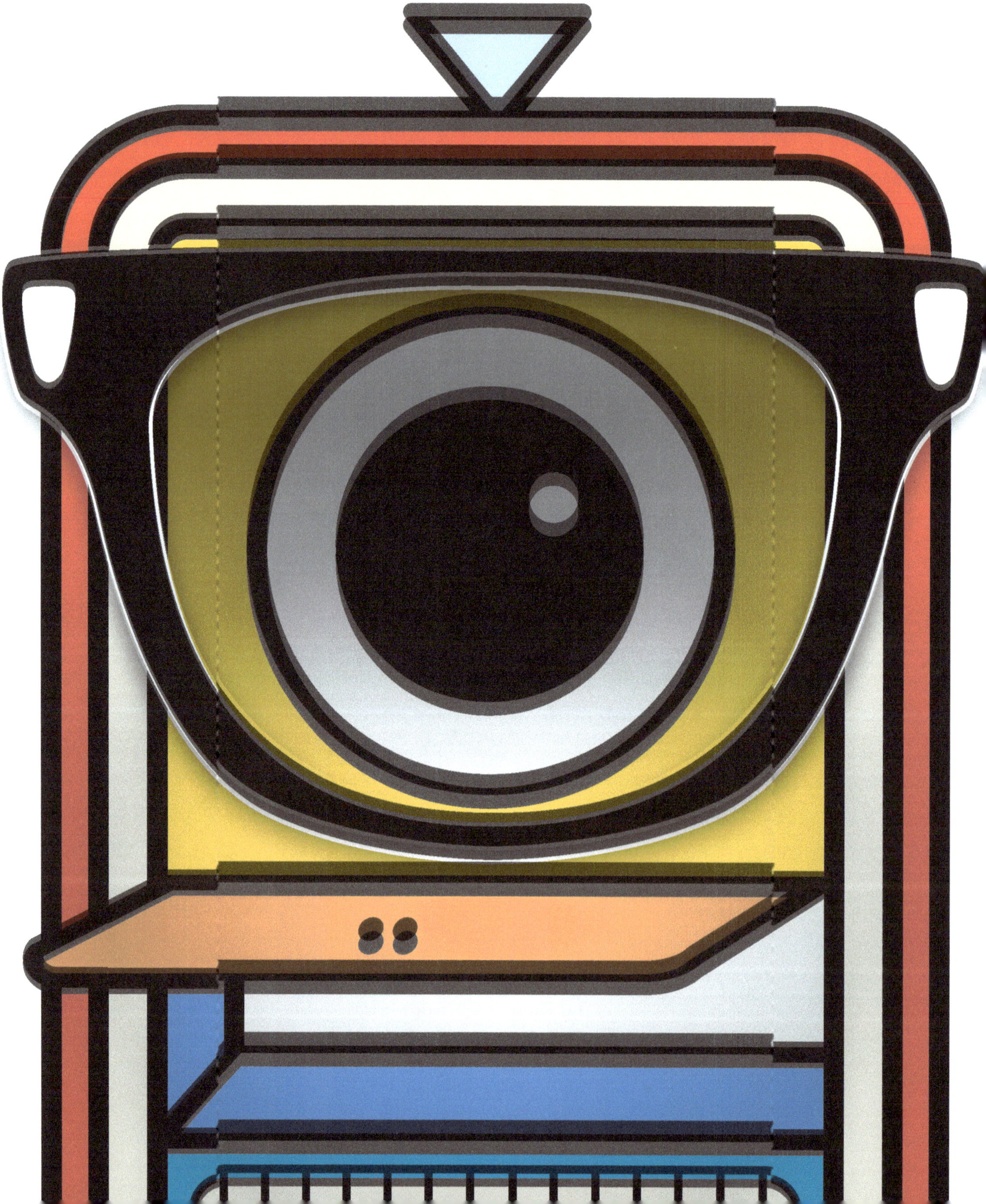

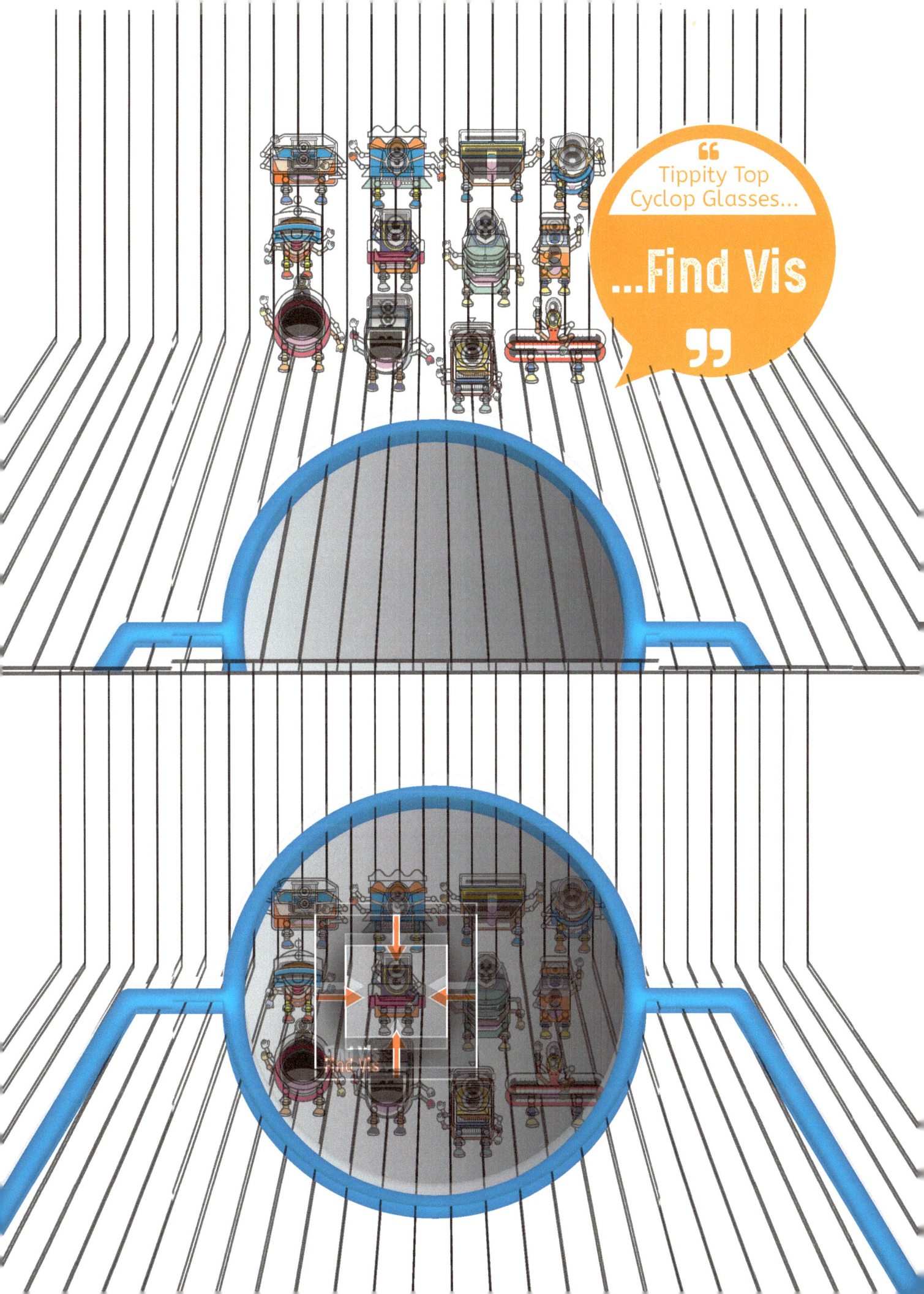

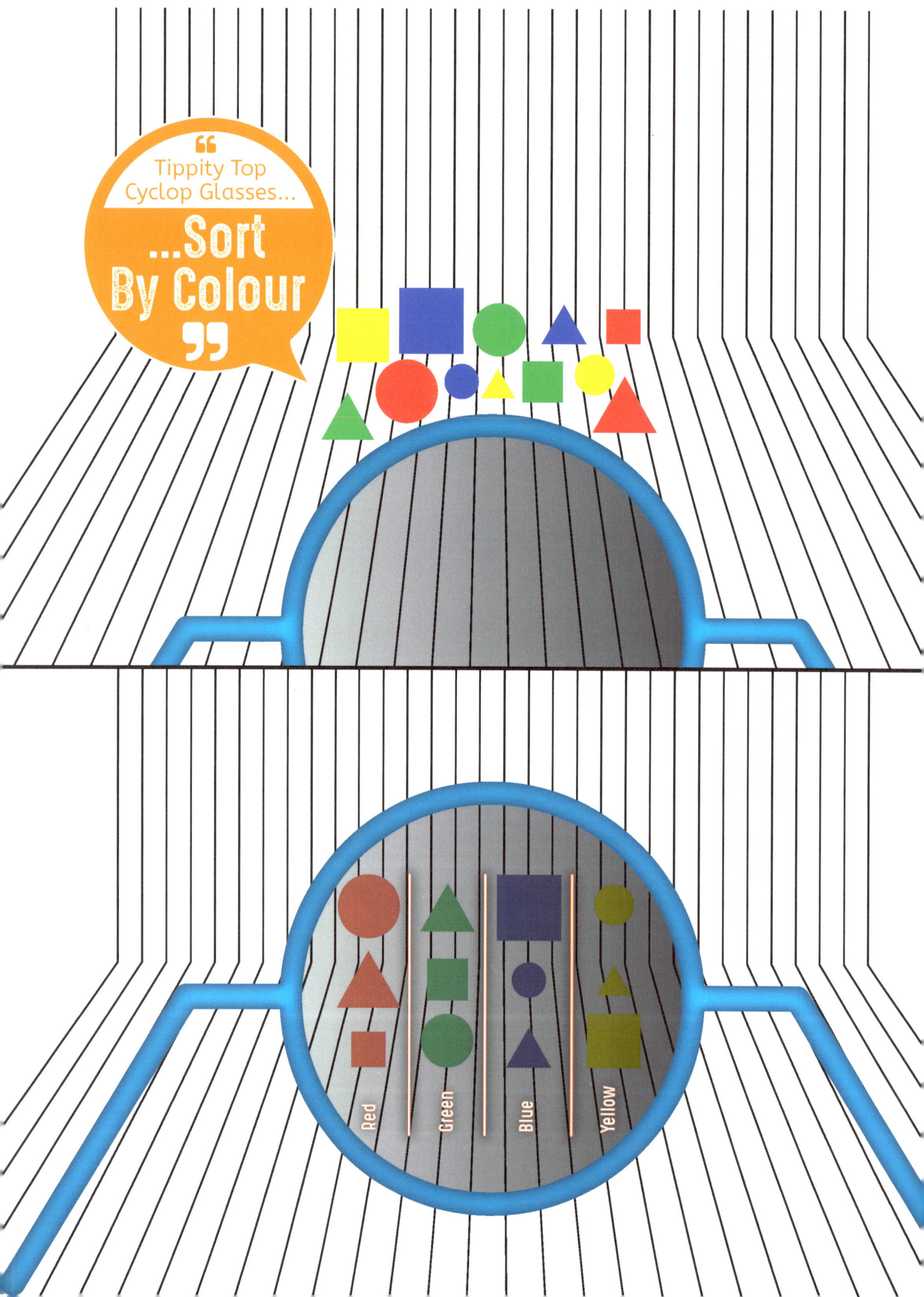

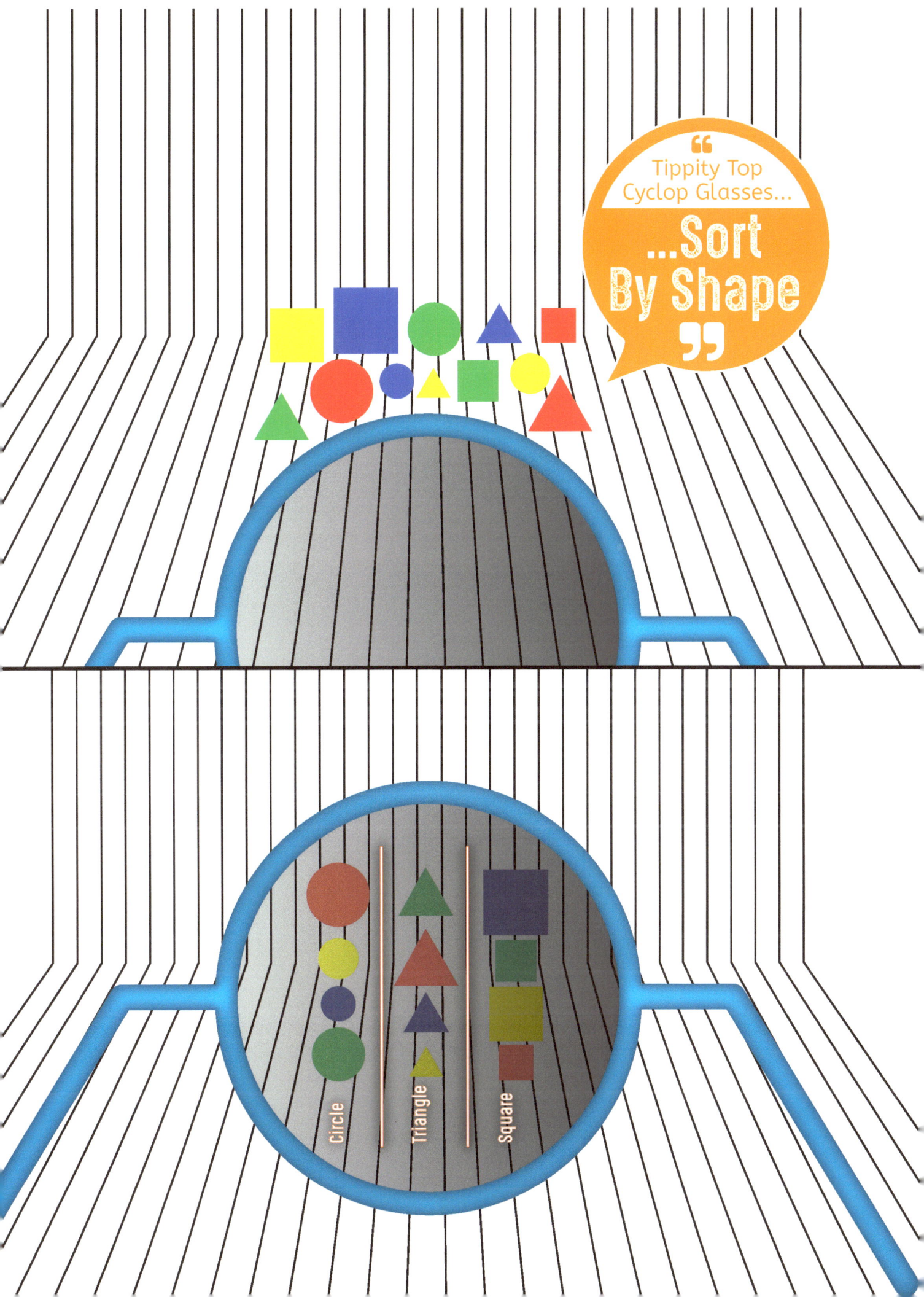

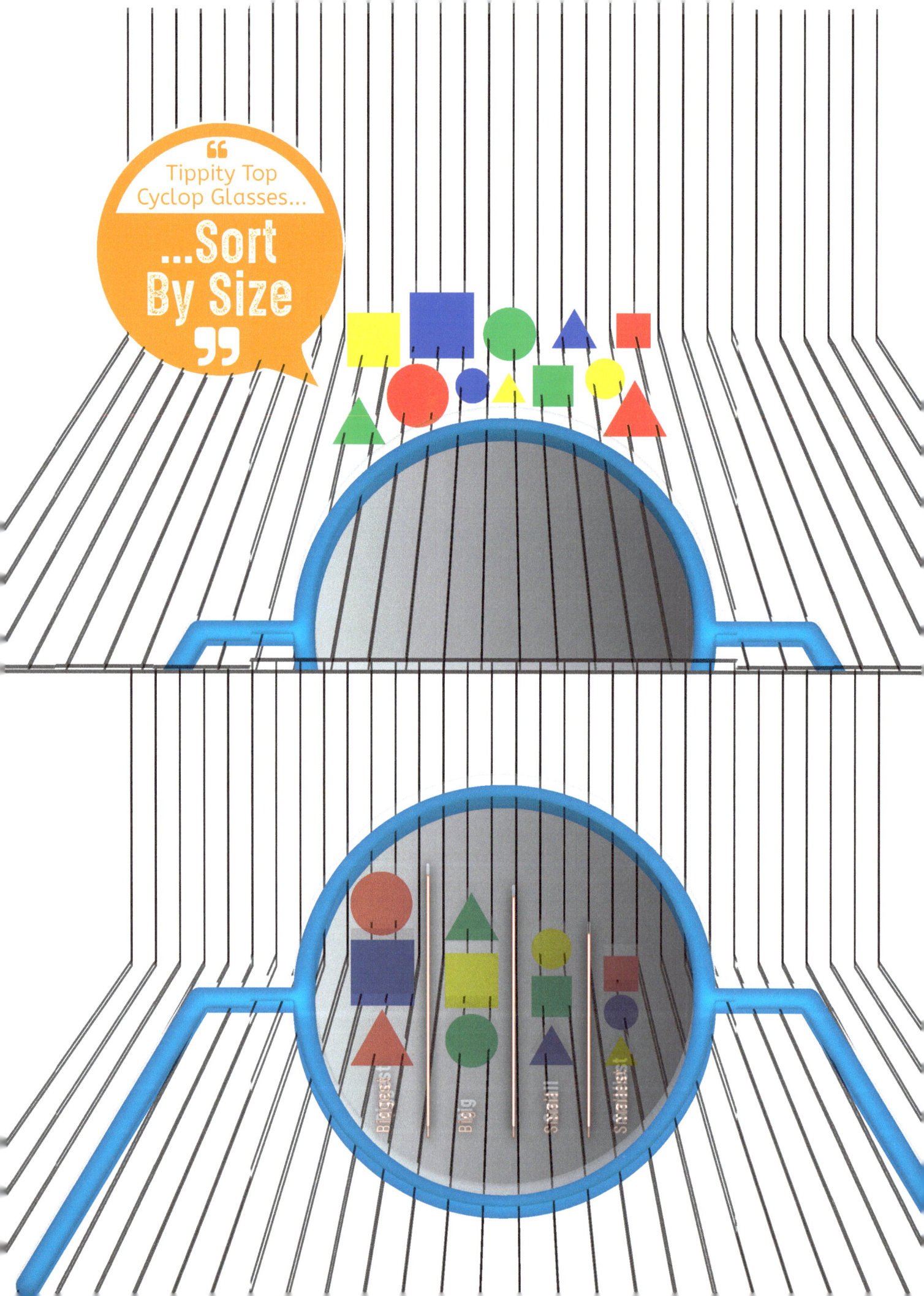

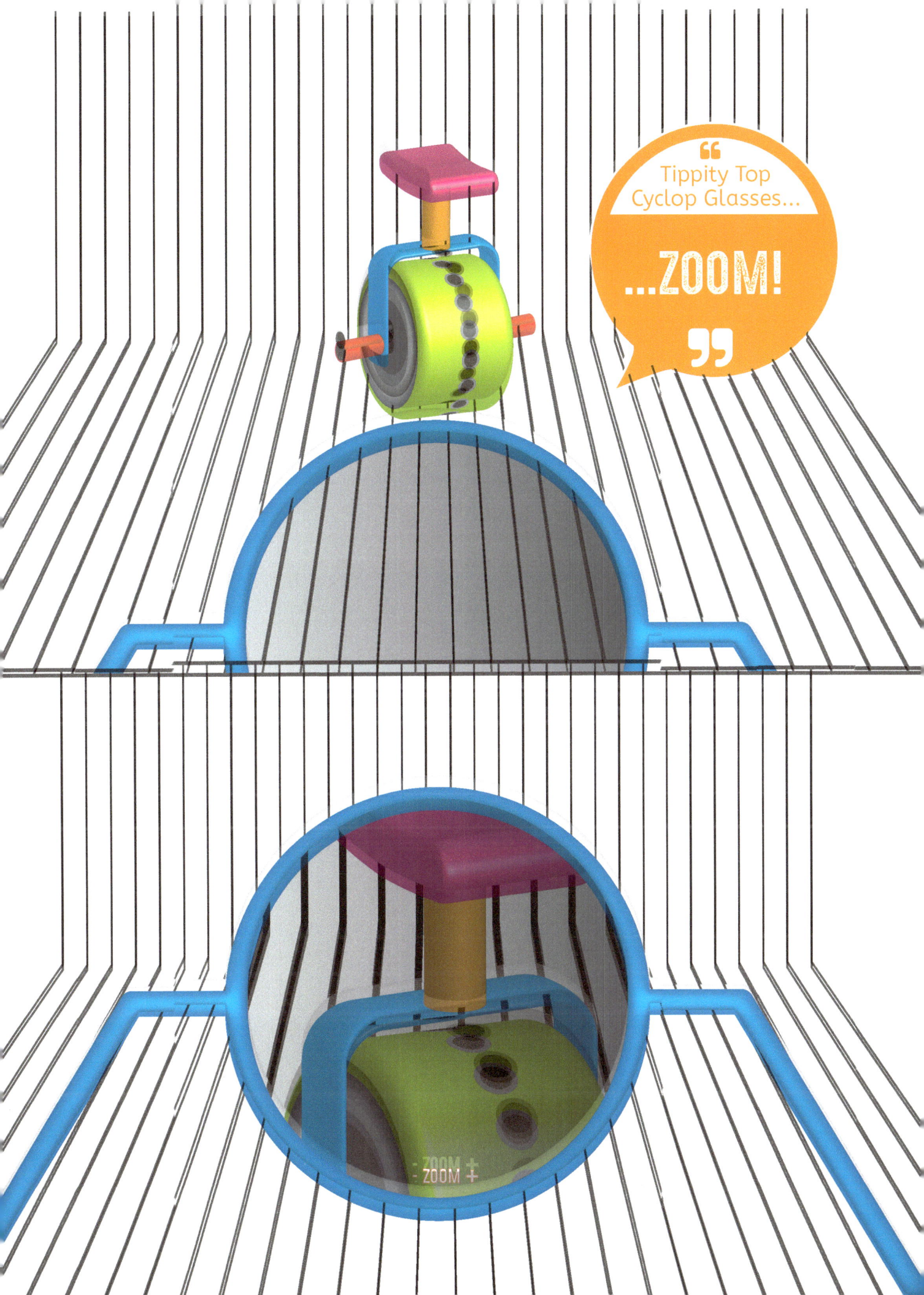

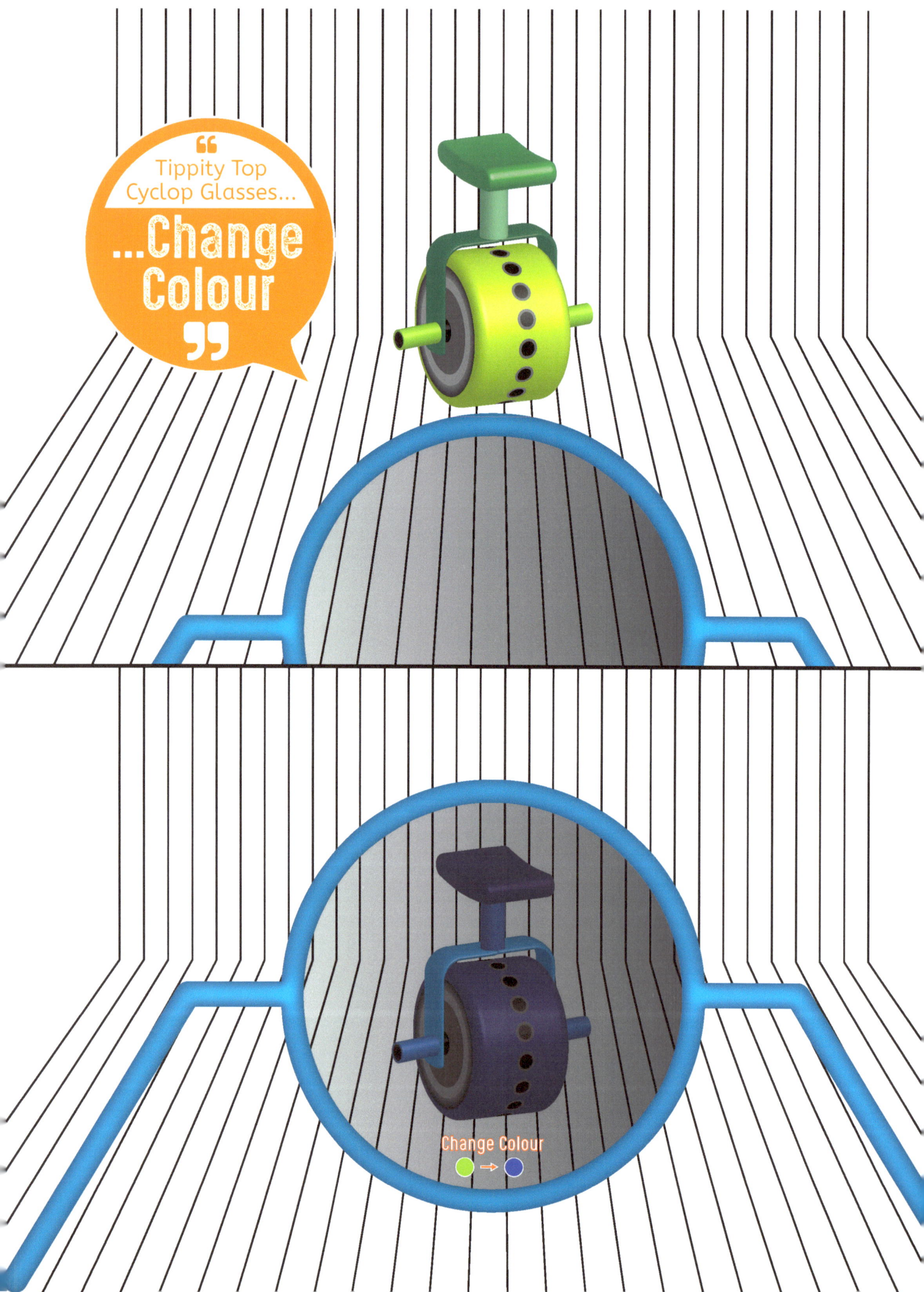

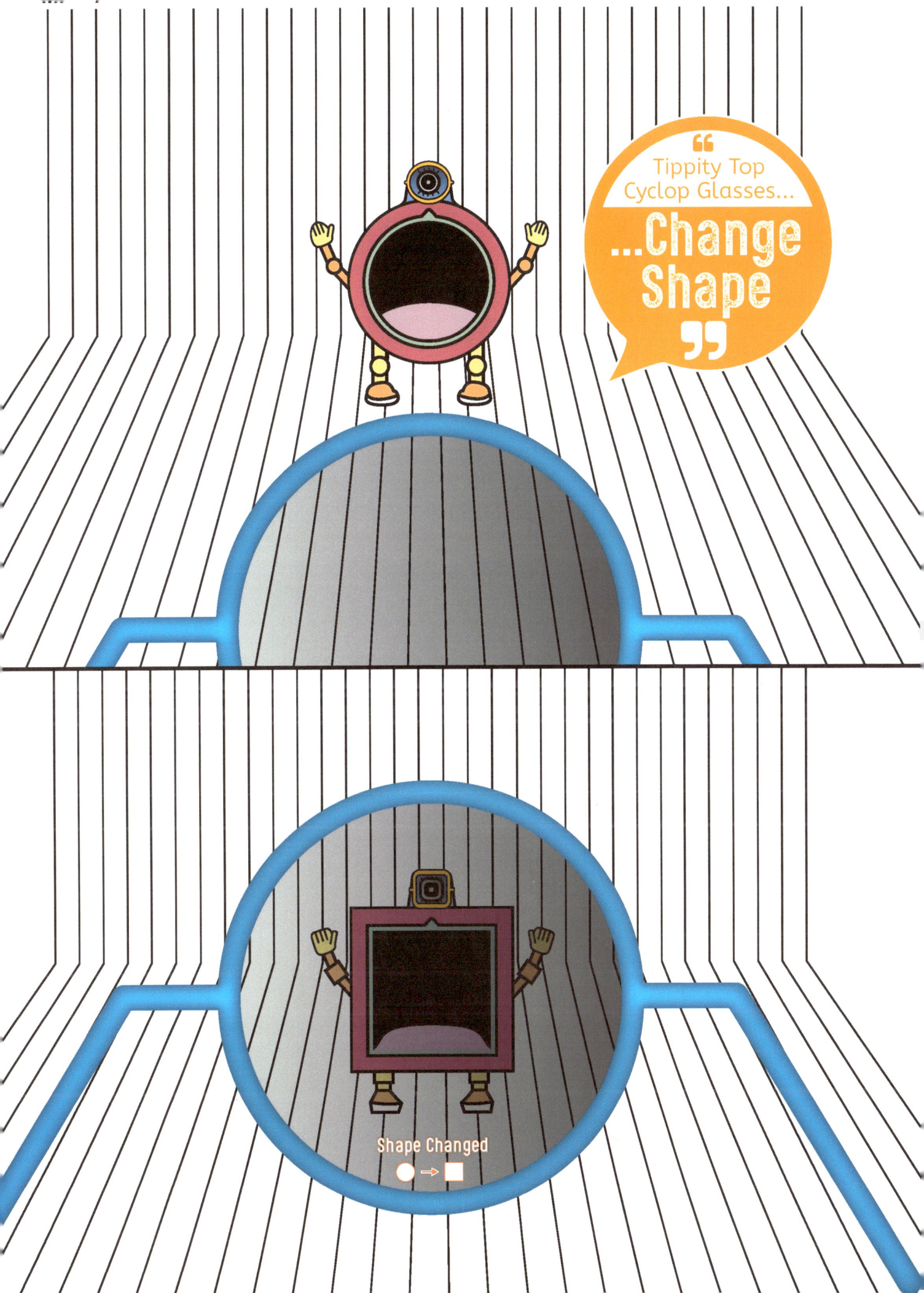

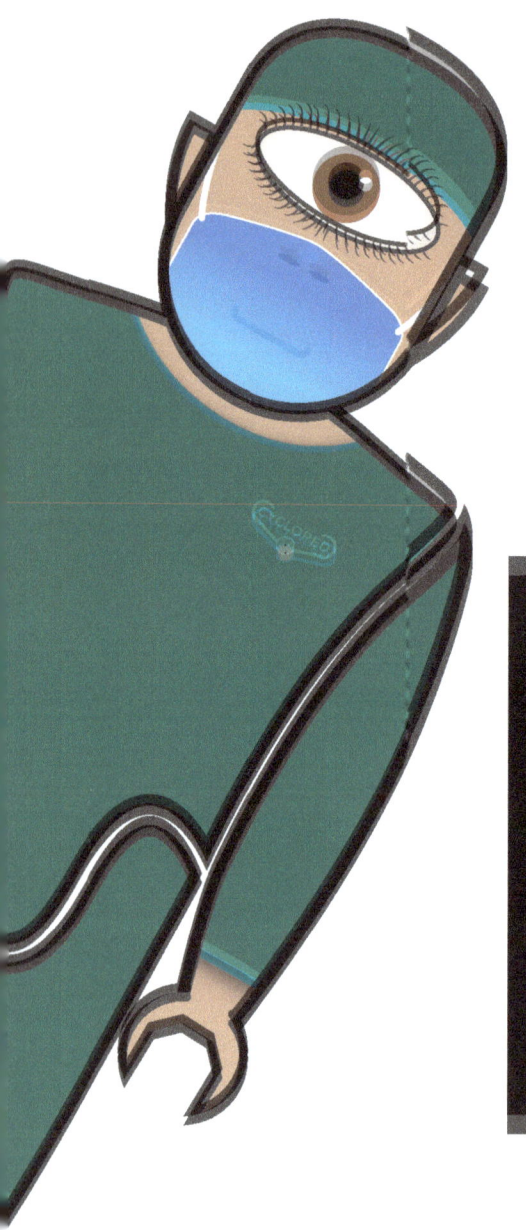

The world's first fictional cosmetic clinic blew peoples minds when they developed their patented 'Cycloped' Eye Reduction Surgery.

The following characters were inspired by some of the fictional patients from Si Klopp Cosmetic Clinic.

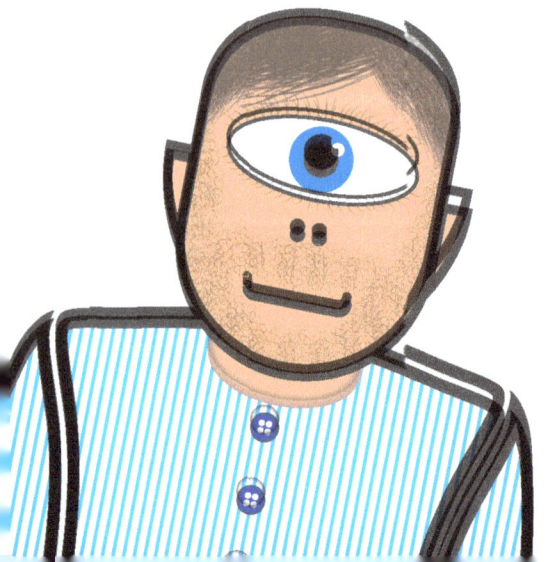
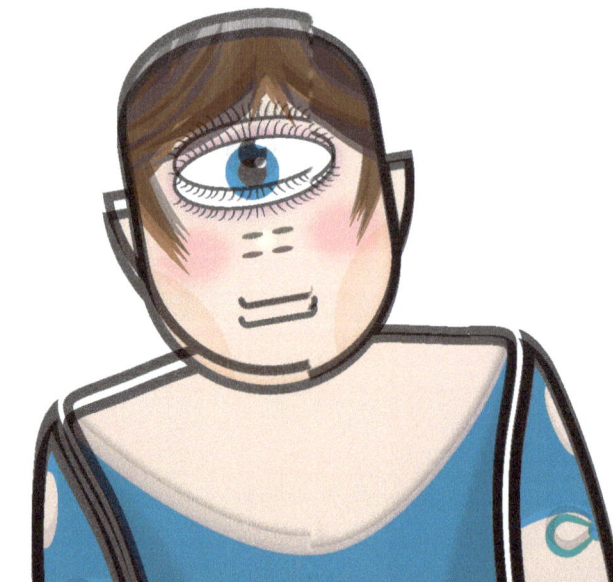

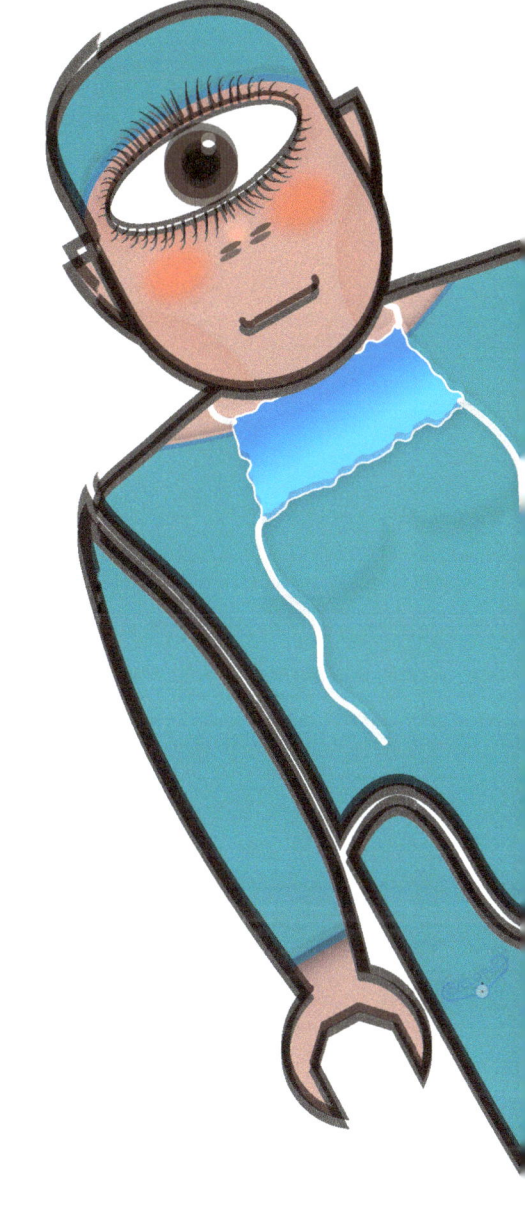
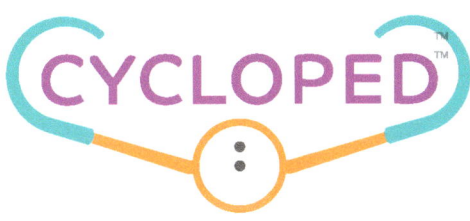
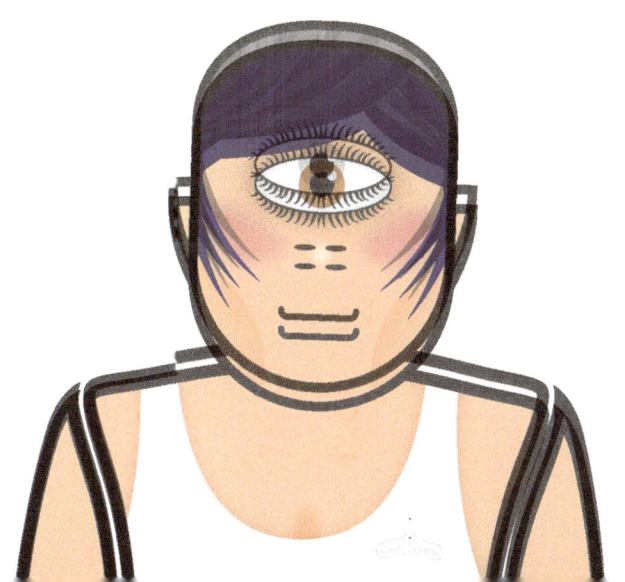
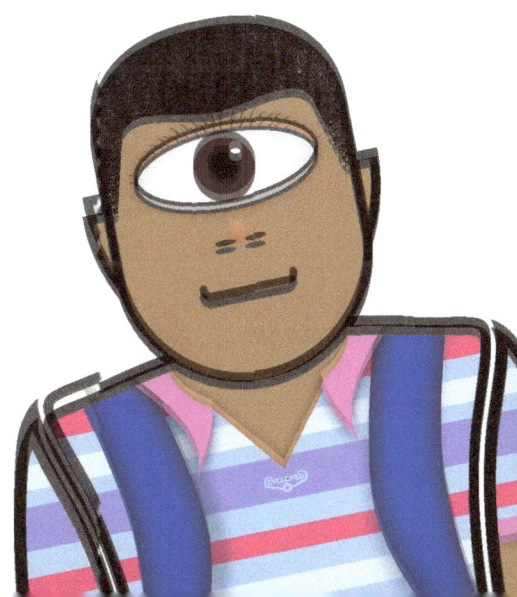

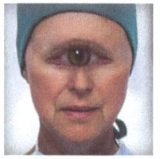

PROFESSOR SIMONE KLOPP

Founder of Si Klopp Cosmetic Surgery and Co-inventor of the patented 'Cycloped' cosmetic procedure.

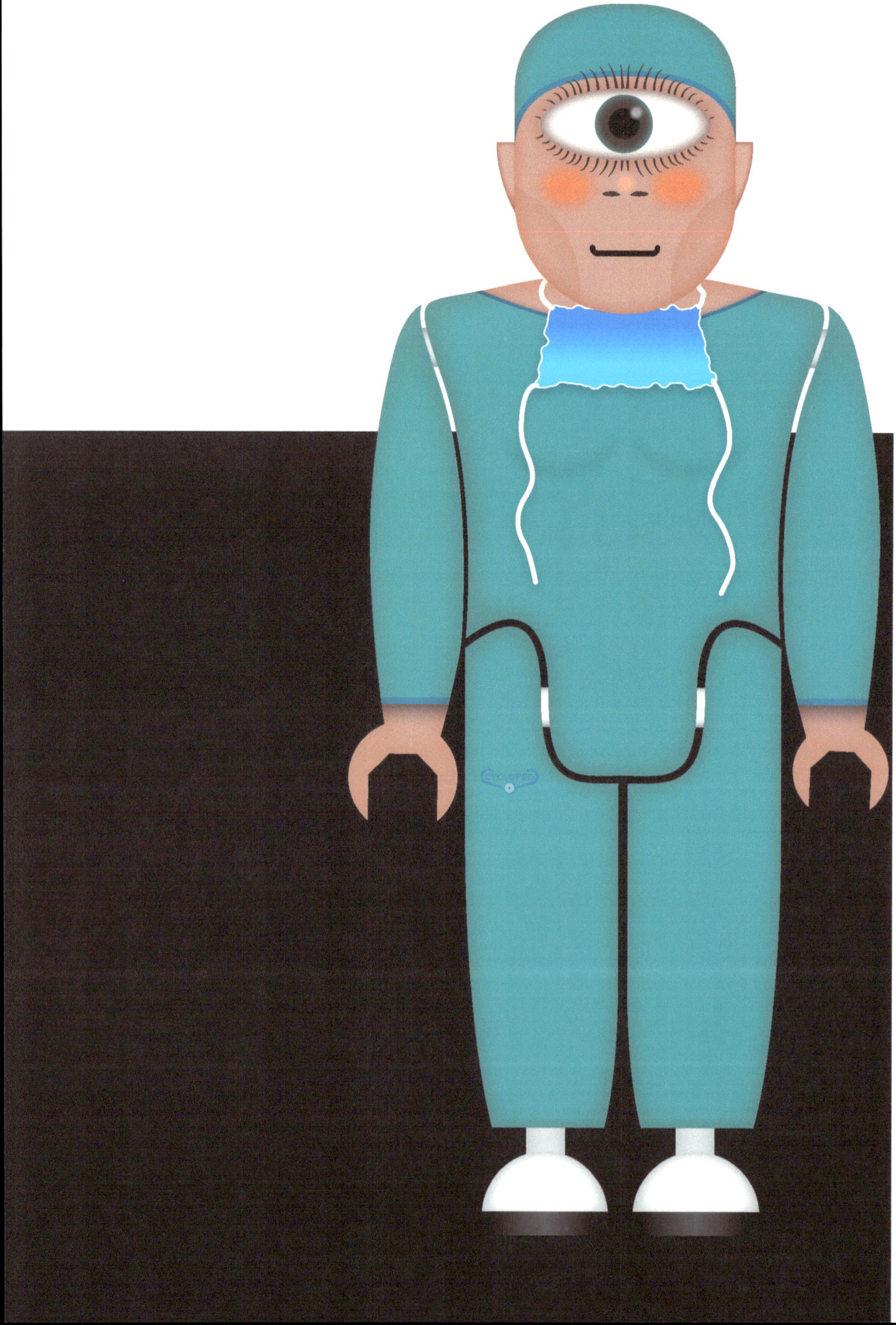

Reason for name:
Simone, preferring to be known as Si for short, means her name sounds like her surgical procedure, Si Klopp (Cyclop).

Simone's Character:
A failing cosmetic surgeon who changed her life, and the world, after becoming inspired to create the 'Cycloped' Eye Reduction Surgery.

Simone is a genius who loves the odd and quirky things in life.

At times, her frustration with the mundane leaves her needing emotional support.

DR VON EYID

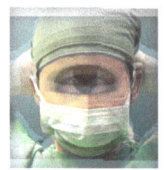

Head Surgeon and Co-inventor of the patented 'Cycloped' cosmetic procedure.

Reason for name:
Dr Von Eyid is a play on the words 'One-Eyed'.

Von's Character:
A risk-taker who became disillusioned with life and the boring world of lip fillers and tummy tucks, instead choosing to work in a morgue where Von used the dead bodies to perfect the 'Cycloped' Eye Reduction Procedure.

At times Von can be reckless in his pursuit of adrenaline dumps and tries to keep this in check by partaking in extreme sports.

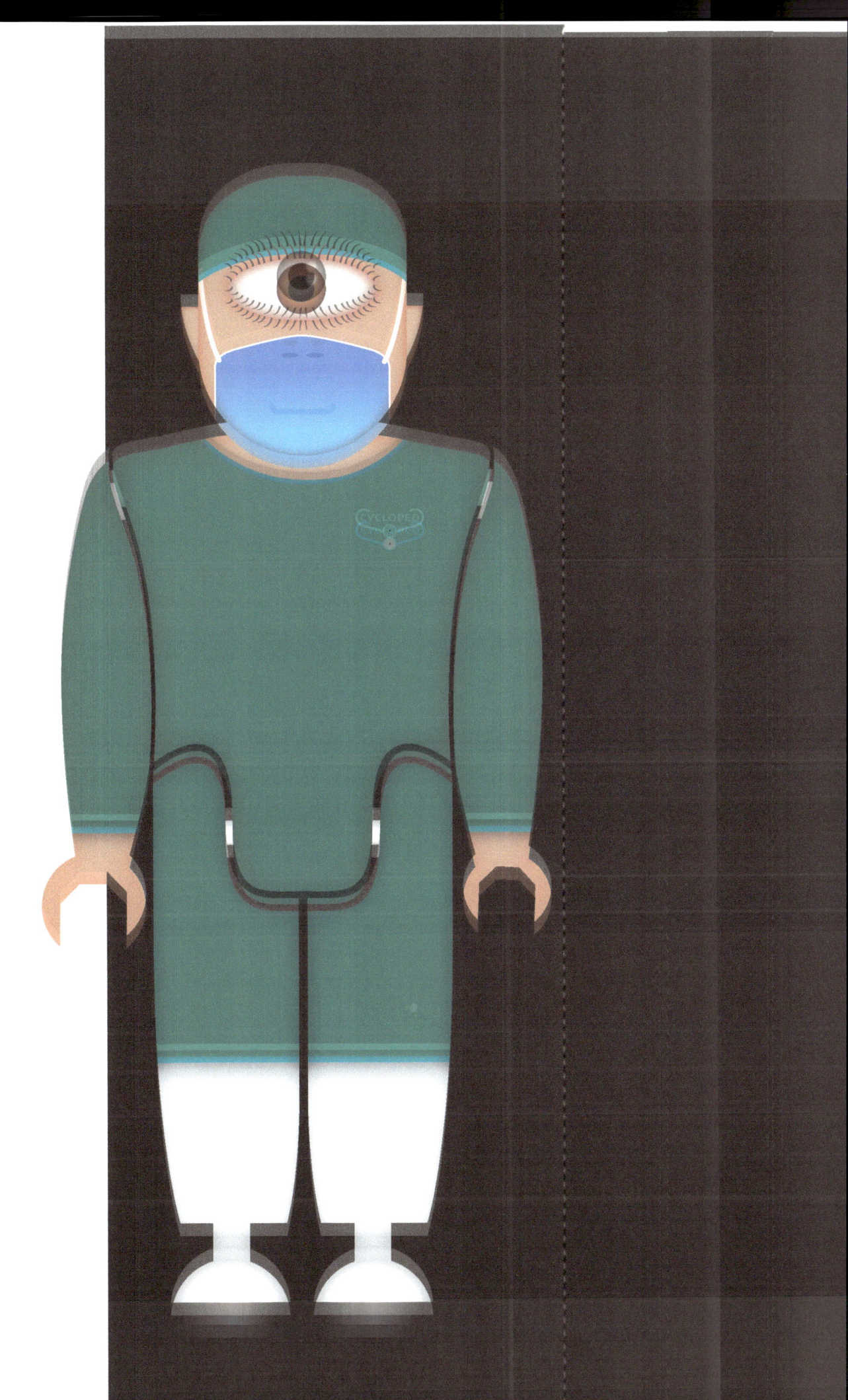

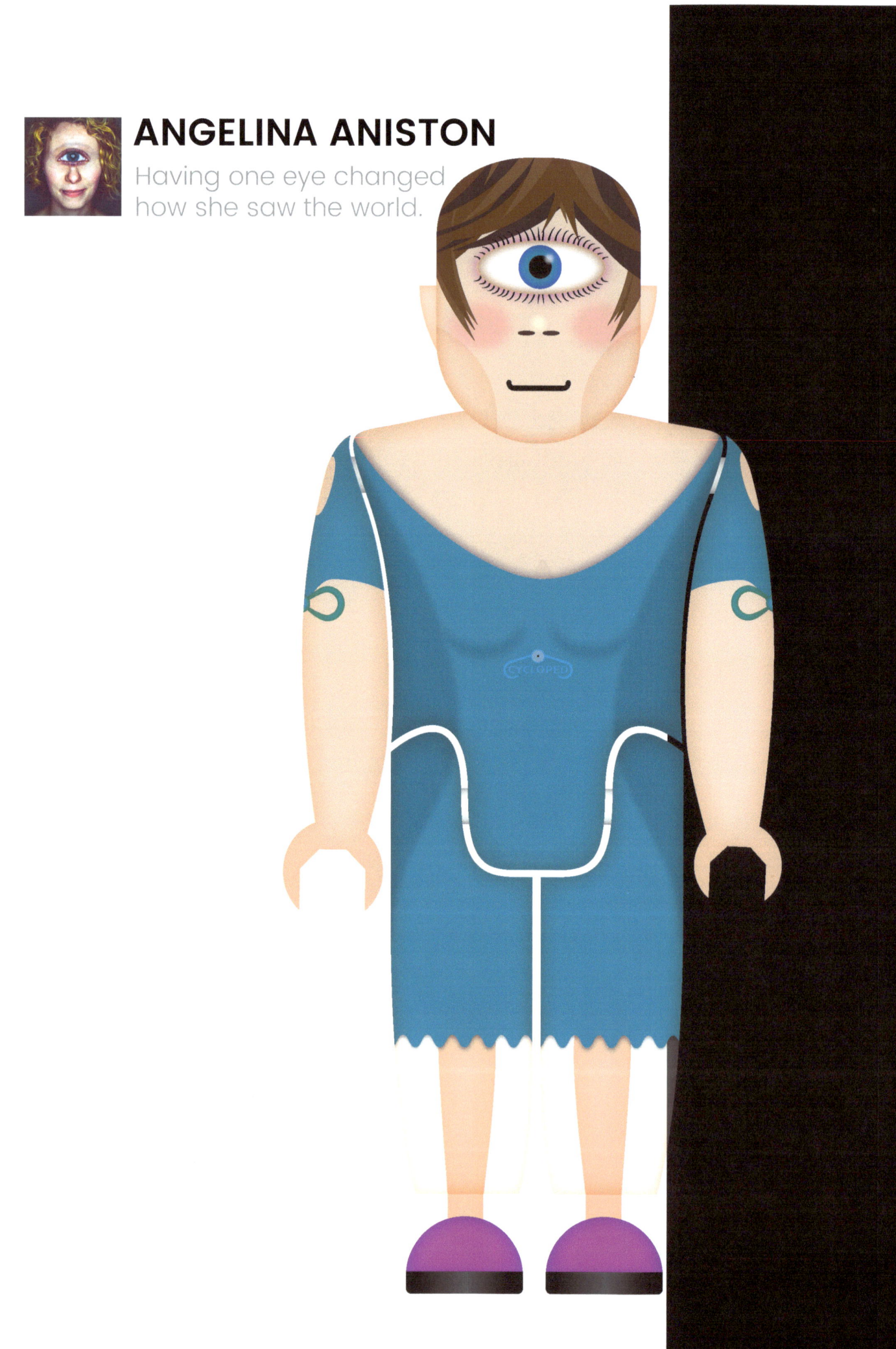

ANGELINA ANISTON
Having one eye changed how she saw the world.

Reason for name:
Angelina Aniston is a mixture of the names Angelina Jolie and Jennifer Aniston.

Angelina's Character:
Rebellious, impulsive and aggressive, yet also a conformist, thoughtful and gentle at times. A living contradiction, you never know which Angelina you will get.

MORGAN WHITAKER

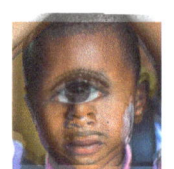

'Cycloped' Eye Reduction surgery saved his life.

Reason for name:
Morgan Whitaker derived from Morgan Freeman's first name and Forest Whitaker's surname.

Morgan's Character:
Morgan is very grateful for every day he has on earth.

Professor Klopp only performs surgery on children when it is required to save their life.

After the discovery of a large growth on Morgan's brain, Simone Klopp kindly performed the surgery free of charge.

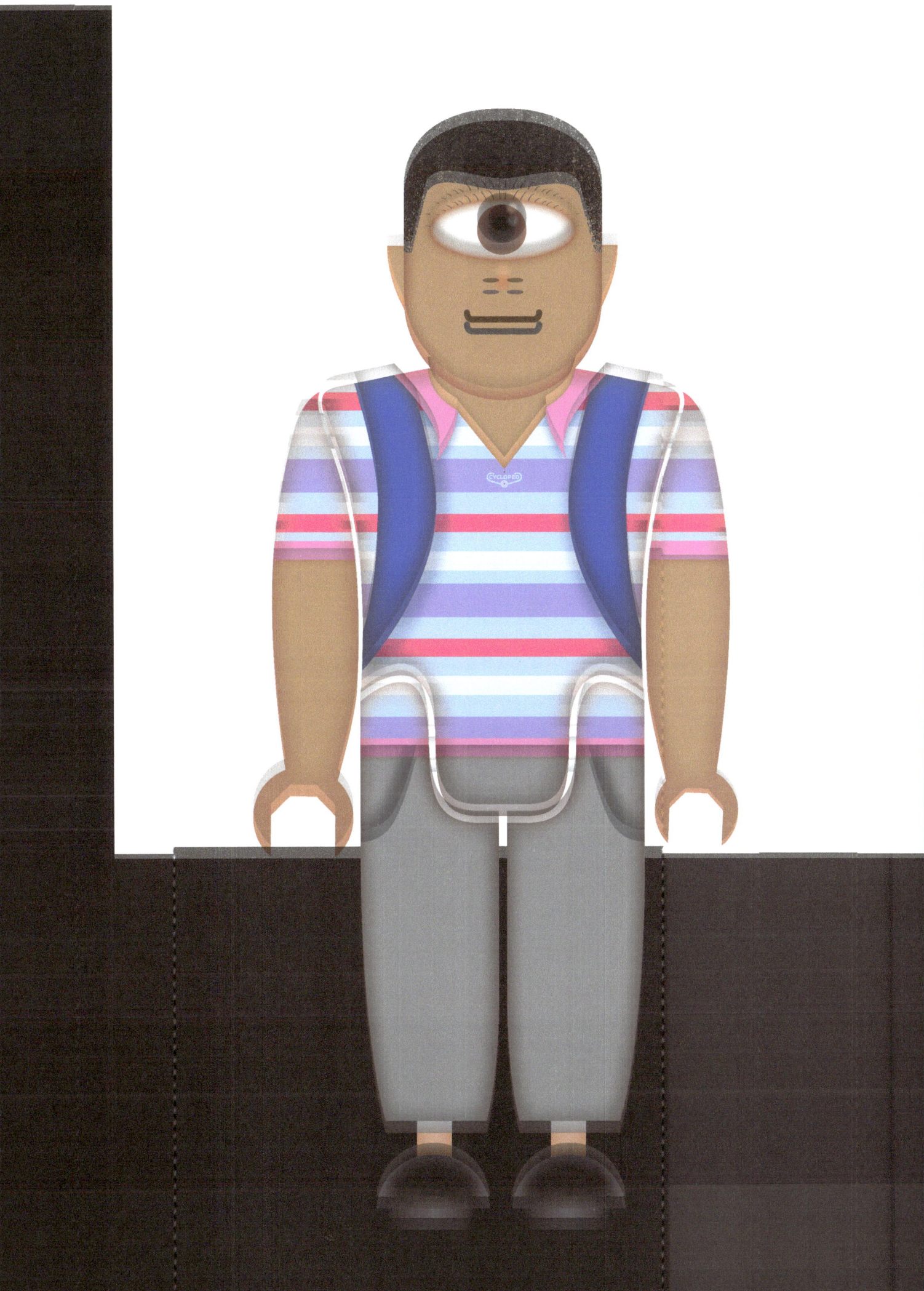

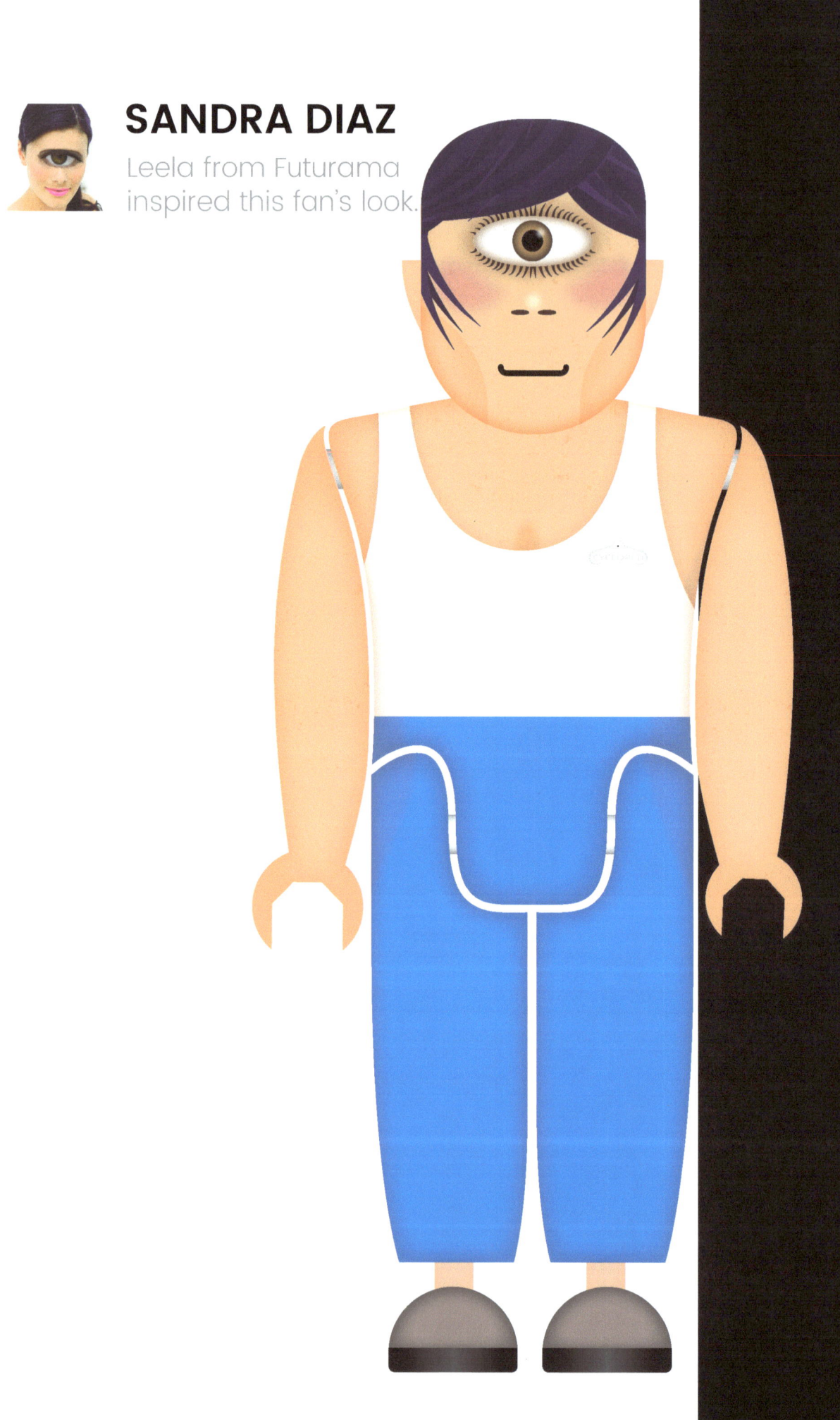

SANDRA DIAZ

Leela from Futurama inspired this fan's look.

Reason for name:
Sandra Diaz is a mixture of Sandra Bullock and Cameron Diaz's names.

Sandra's Character:
Becoming very wealthy through an unexpected inheritance, Sandra's money worries disappeared.

Self-obsessed, she uses her wealth to purchase whatever she wants and to attend comic conferences around the world.

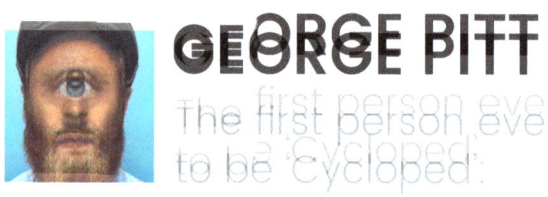

GEORGE PITT

The first person ever to be 'Cycloped'.

Reason for name:

George Pitt is a mixture of George Clooney's first name and Brad Pitt's surname.

George's Character:

Always loving to be first, George is one of life's winners. He somehow manages to always come out on top without ever having to try.

When things do not go his way, George finds it difficult to accept and is prone to child-like tantrums, much like the one he may have after realising he is the last characters to be introduced in this book.

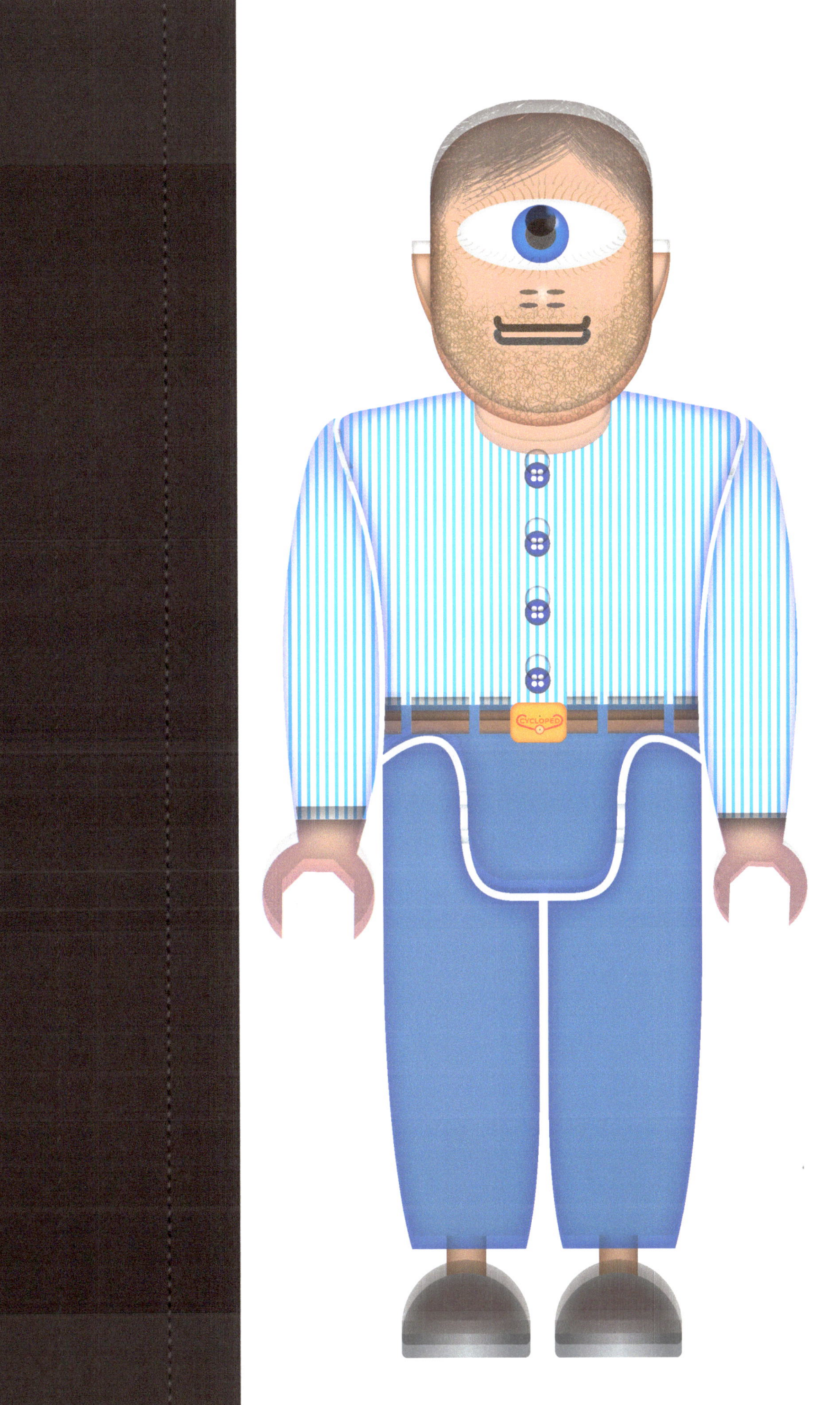

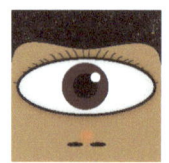 **'CYCLOPED' TOY CONCEPT**
Replicating Eye Reduction Surgery, Pressing the ears will spin and change the two-eyed toy into a Cyclop.

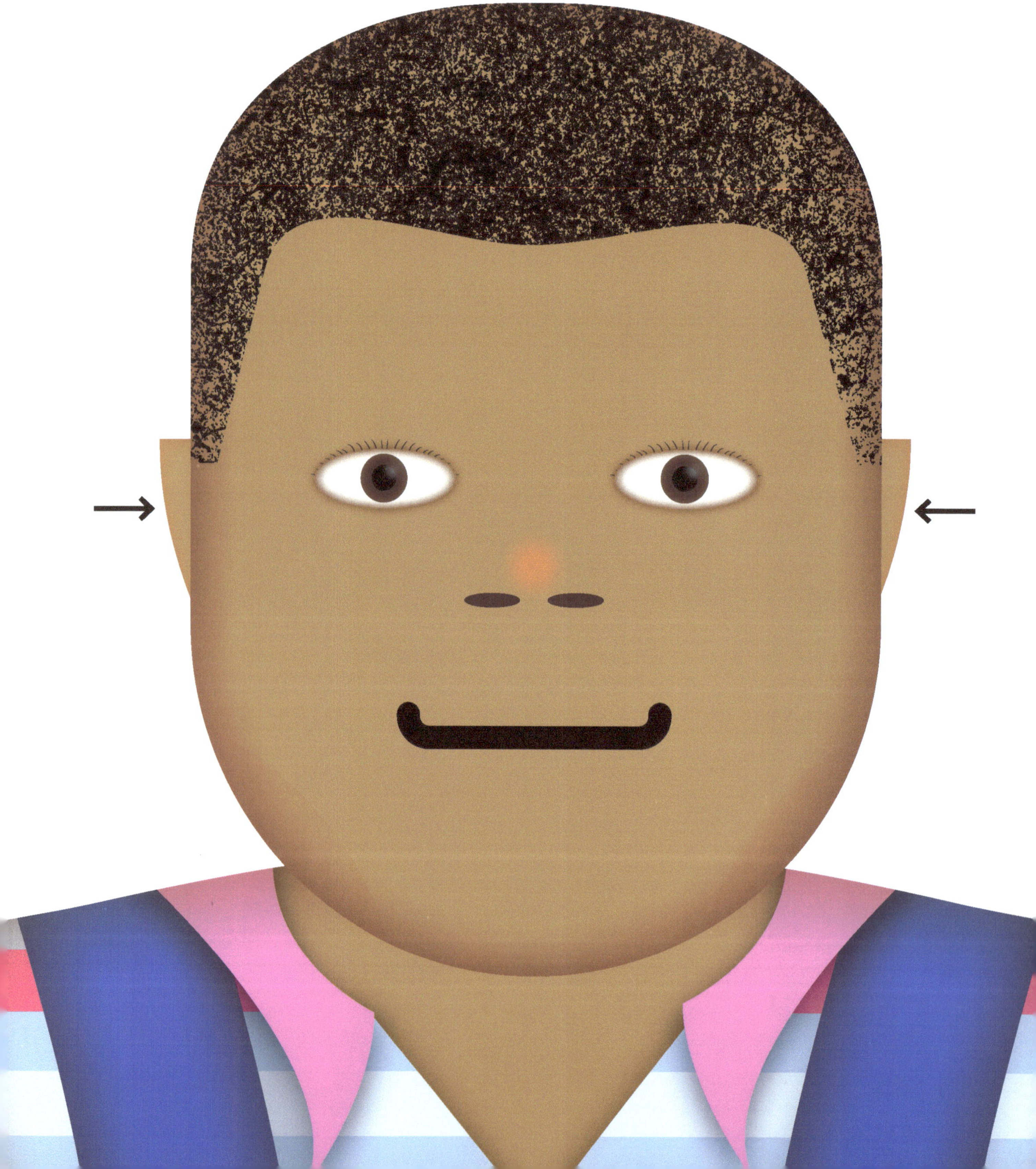

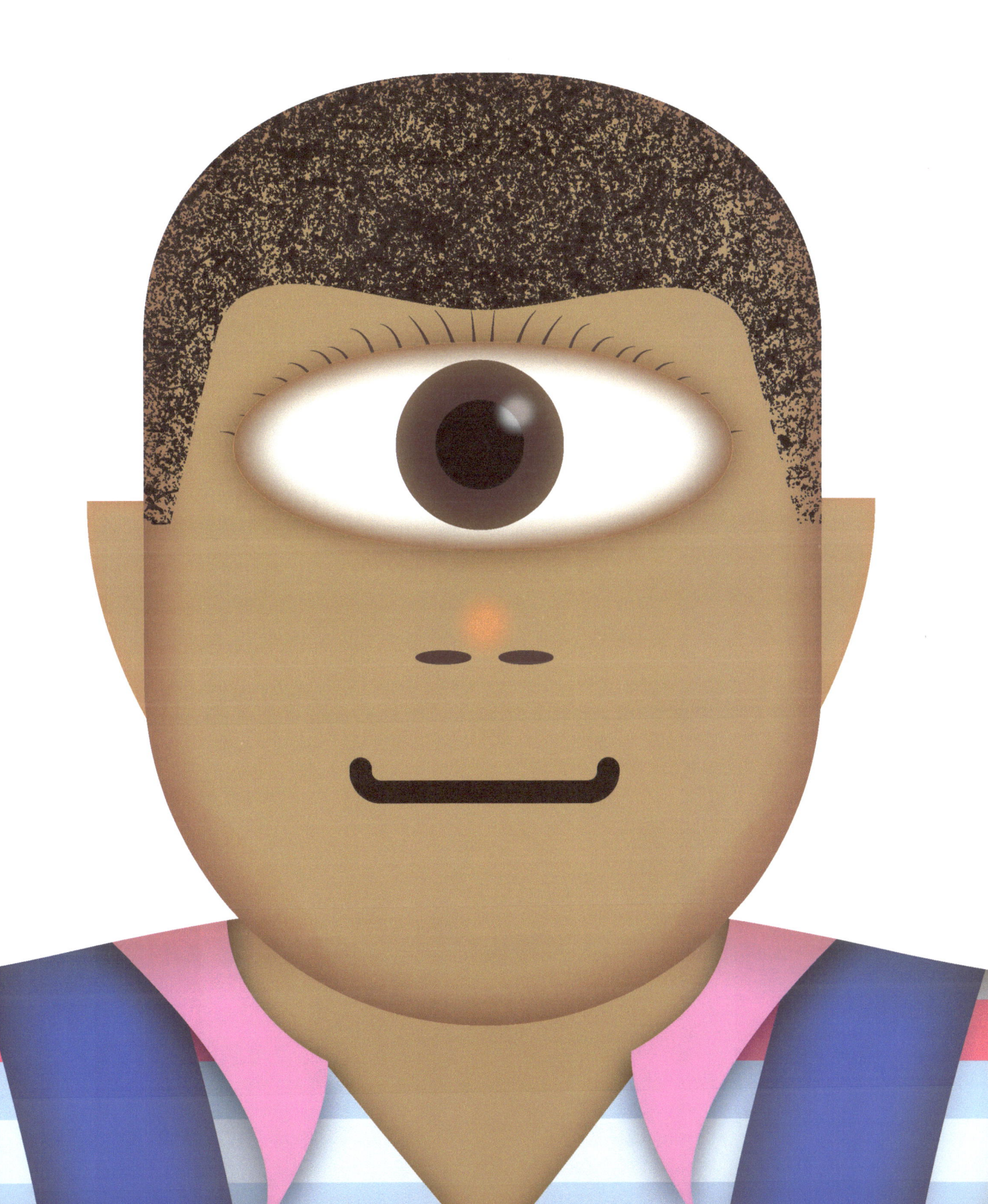

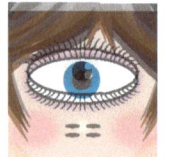

VARIOUS SIZES AND PATTERNS

Just like Be@rBricks, the toys would be created in a variety of sizes and painted to depcited different characters.

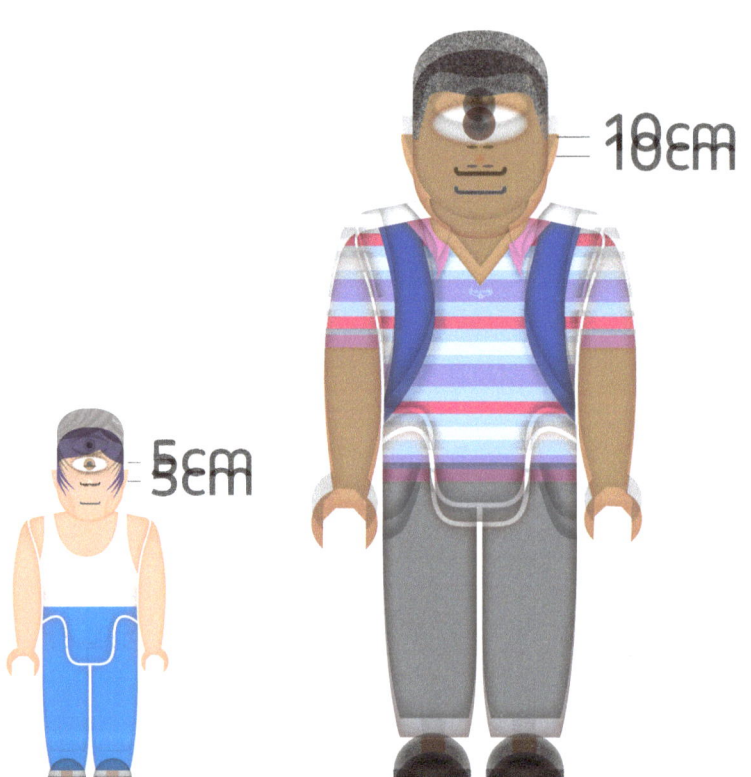

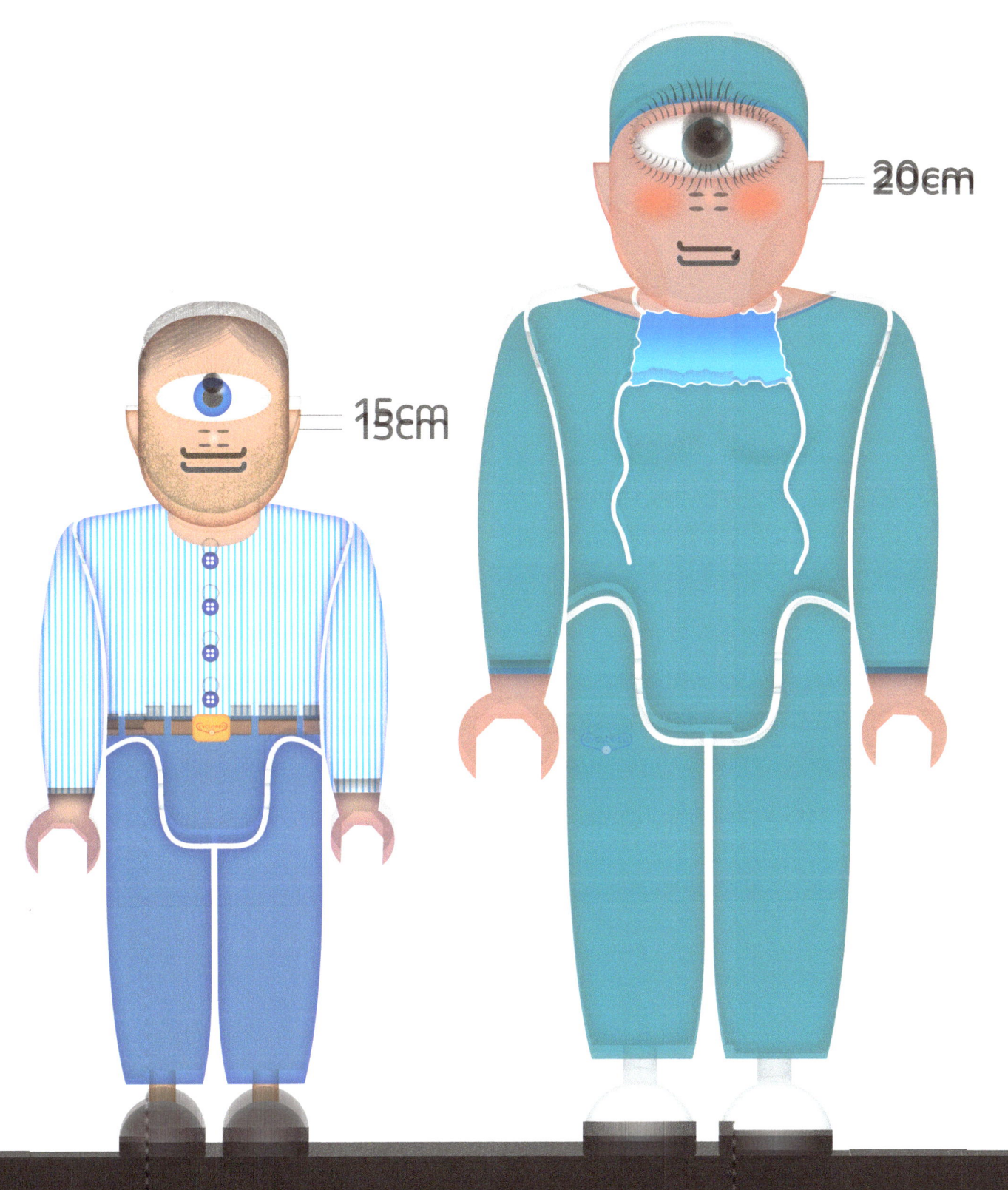

www.R-and-Q.com

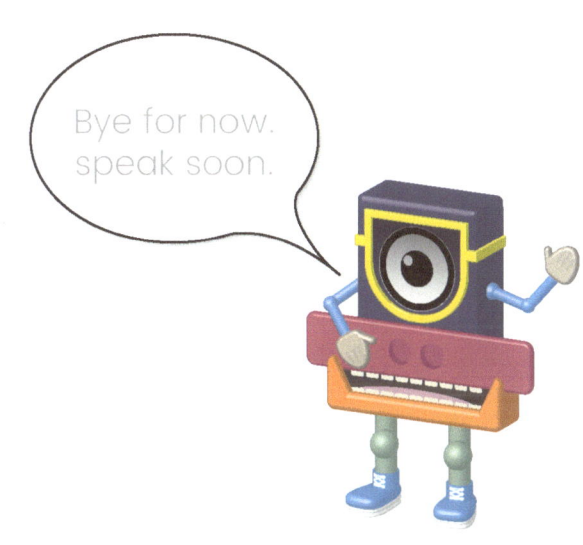

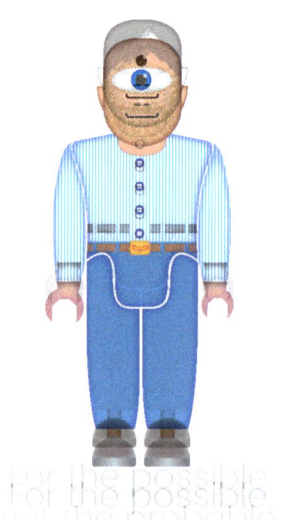